NEW WAYS TO
·EAT·WELL·

Copyright © Bay Books

Published by Bay Books
61–69 Anzac Parade,
Kensington NSW 2033

Publisher: George Barber

National Library of Australia
Card Number and ISBN 1 86256 267 9

ACKNOWLEDGEMENTS

The publisher would like to thank the following for providing cutlery, glassware and tableware for the photography of this book.
Accoutrement for tableware (pages 24, 28, 30, 31)
Bridget Hancock for glassware (pages 45, 46, 52, 53, 57, 61, 64, 78, 79)
Dansab for tableware (pages 36, 38, 39, 49, 54, 68, 70, 71, 76, 77, 79, 80, 81, 86, 87, 89, 91, 92, 93)
Made Where for tableware (pages 31, 34, 36, 44)
Pochoir Gallery for glassware (pages 37, 40, 41, 48, 66, 67)
The Warren Tippet Workshop for tableware (pages 7, 35)

BBC 88/87/86/85

Printed in Singapore by Toppan Printing Co. (S) Pty. Ltd.

Photography Ashley Barber
Styling Michelle Gorry

NEW WAYS TO
·EAT·WELL·

Compiled by Susan Tomnay

BAY BOOKS
SYDNEY AND LONDON

CONTENTS

INTRODUCTION

There's a quiet revolution going on in food. People, more health-conscious than ever, are eating smaller, lighter, fresher meals. More women working outside the home mean that there's less time available for preparing meals. Gone are the two or three big courses. A family meal now might consist of two or three dishes eaten together that once were considered simply as first courses or vegetable dishes, soup and salad, or soup and bread with fresh fruit and cheese after. Even when entertaining, the big lavish three course meal is out.

This change in eating habits means you can still eat what you like without forfeiting the waistline. Dieting isn't about a main meal of a single lettuce leaf but, instead, a commonsense approach to food and an awareness of its nutritional values. Eating should fit into your lifestyle, not dominate and inhibit it as can be the case when following a fad diet.

That's why this book is heavy on first courses and salads and rather light on meats. It's not a vegetarian cookbook, but it's a book that understands the mood of the times. People are, in the main, still eating meat, but they're eating it less often, or in smaller quantities. The recipes in this book have been designed for healthy eating while also being interesting and fun!

Meatless main courses, often based on grains or pulses, are well represented. The dessert chapter is small, however there's a section on unusual fruits, mostly tropical, which are now available in some fruit markets. Fruit is the easiest dessert, the quickest, the healthiest, and except in the dead of winter, when you crave something hot and sweet, the most delicious.

Good health depends on eating the right amount of the right kind of food, and eating a variety of food. Base your diet on complex carbohydrates in the form of grains,

pulses, vegetables and fruit, eat a smaller amount of protein in the form of meat, fish, poultry, dairy foods and nuts, and an even smaller amount of fats, in the form of butter and oil. And vary your diet — if you want fried fish one night, have it, if you want cream in your soup, go right ahead. Just don't have it every night.

If you make sure that fibre-rich grains, pulses and vegetables are the mainstay of your diet, a splurge on rich, fatty food now and again isn't going to hurt. That's why these foods are included in the book. The food you eat should make you happy, not bored.

In the sixties when people were just starting to think about getting healthy, the gurus of the time didn't even mention fibre. They talked about protein, mostly meat, as the most important part of the diet, to maintain health and build new cells. Carbohydrates were thought of as simply energy foods.

Later research indicated that too much fat and high levels of cholesterol caused heart disease and that fibre was an important element in our diet. Primitive tribes who existed on grains, pulses, fruit and vegetables and showed no signs of the common illnesses that systematically kill us in the 'civilised' world were examined. Meat, which contains fat and hardly any fibre became the bad guy.

Complex carbohydrates started looking good. They are low in fats, high in fibre and produce energy and endurance. Athletes who previously would have eaten a large steak before a race now win on a bowl of pasta and vegetables.

But a body can't exist on carbohydrates alone. Proteins must be included in the diet too, and so should fats, but in moderation. The key to good health is variety.

FIBRE

The foods listed above also supply fibre, much needed by the body for effective elimination.

PROTEIN

We get protein from meat, fish, poultry, eggs, nuts and dairy products. As much as possible eat lean meat; trim most of the fat off before you cook it. Replace whole milk, cream, sour cream and butter with healthier and just as tasty equivalents: skim milk, low-fat yoghurt and low-fat margarine.

Vegetarians should regularly eat pulses and grains together to ensure they get enough protein.

CARBOHYDRATES

We get carbohydrates from grains in the form of wholewheat bread, cereals, pasta and rice; from pulses (dried beans, peas and lentils) and from fruit and vegetables. These are all high in fibre and low in fat. Nuts are carbohydrates too, but they are high in fat.

If you really want to keep those kilojoules down one handy hint is to use pureed vegetables rather than flour for thickening sauces, gravies, etc.

Grains and pulses also supply protein, but they are called incomplete protein because singly, with the exception of soybeans, they do not supply all the amino acids necessary for forming new cells. However, if grains and pulses are eaten at the same meal, the amino acids missing from one are made up by the other. That's why primitive cultures who exist on rice and lentils are so healthy.

FATS

Generally we eat far too much fat. We get it from butter, other whole milk dairy foods and oil. One tablespoon of oil will supply our day's fat requirement. When using meat stock, try to always refrigerate it first. The fat can then be easily removed.

VITAMINS AND MINERALS

If we eat a variety of the foods listed above in the proportion of mainly carbohydrates, a smaller amount of protein and a minimum of fats, we'll get enough vitamins and minerals.

SALT

Try to cook your vegetables without salt, and only salt those foods that you just can't enjoy without it. If you eat a lot of processed and junk food, you should avoid salt altogether in your home cooking. Some vegetables, notably eggplant and zucchini, are salted and left to drain for half an hour or so before they are cooked. The salt draws out the bitter juices that these vegetables develop, especially when they are large. Rinse the salt off in cold running water and dry the vegetables with paper towels before cooking.

GRAINS

Grains: Energy food high in vitamins and low in fat.

GRAINS

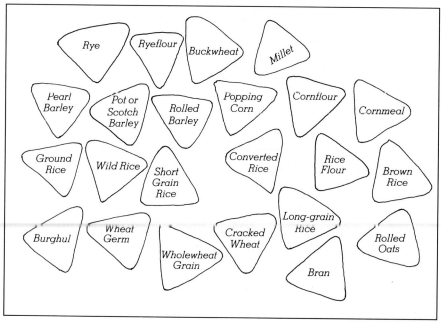

Grains are the most important part of most of the world's cuisine. They keep more than half of the population alive. Grains contain carbohydrates and are an excellent source of dietary fibre. They are low in fat, contain no cholesterol, and are valuable suppliers of B vitamins, iron and calcium. Grains are called 'incomplete protein', because they don't contain all the amino acids necessary to rebuild cells. Pulses are also incomplete protein. But pulses contain the amino acids missing from grains and so when they are eaten together, they form a balanced diet.

Many people don't eat grains in the form of bread or pasta or rice because they believe grains are fattening. However, it's not the grains that are heavy in kilojoules, it's what you have with them. Butter and jam on bread, creamy sauces on pasta, fried rice, will all add kilos, but it's the fat, not the grains, that are doing it.

The image diagram labels the following grains: Rye, Ryeflour, Buckwheat, Millet, Pearl Barley, Pot or Scotch Barley, Rolled Barley, Popping Corn, Cornflour, Cornmeal, Ground Rice, Wild Rice, Short Grain Rice, Converted Rice, Rice Flour, Brown Rice, Burghul, Wheat Germ, Wholewheat Grain, Cracked Wheat, Long-grain Rice, Bran, Rolled Oats

Oats

In Britain and America coarse, medium and fine oatmeal are readily available. In Australia they can sometimes be found in health food shops. But rolled oats are much more common. Rolled oats is oatmeal that has been steamed and flattened between rollers. It is normally used to make porridge and muesli, but can also be added to breads and biscuits.

Buckwheat

Buckwheat grows in northern Europe and is used extensively in Russia. Kasha, a kind of Russian gruel served with meat dishes, is made from buckwheat; so are blinis, pancakes eaten with caviar.

Millet

This can be eaten cooked and eaten in the same way as rice, but millet absorbs much more water than rice does. Millet is the mainstay of the diet in parts of Africa where it is made into flattish breads.

RYE

Rye is commonly used in Germany, Scandinavia and Russia. Its tough kernel should be cracked with a rolling pin and soaked in water before being cooked. It can be boiled until tender and then added to stews or mixed with rice.

Rye Flour

This is used to make black bread and rye crispbreads. Bread made solely from rye flour is very heavy, and most of the rye breads we know are made from a mixture of rye and wheat flours.

RICE

Rice can be cooked in two ways: boiled in plenty of water, or cooked by the absorption method when 3 parts cold water are added to 1 part rice, brought to the boil, covered, and simmered very slowly until the water has been absorbed and the rice is tender.

Short Grain Rice

An all-purpose rice, used for risotto and in desserts.

Long Grain Rice

This is the best rice to use when you want separate grains, for salads, pilafs and as an accompaniment to curries.

Brown Rice

This is natural unpolished rice that has been hulled but has not lost its bran. It takes longer to cook than white rice but can be used in the same way.

Converted Rice

This is rice that has been steam-treated to reduce its cooking time. It is just as nutritious as ordinary rice because it is processed before it is hulled, which means it can absorb the bran's nutrients before the bran is discarded.

Wild Rice

This is not rice at all, but a seed from an aquatic grass which grows in North America. It has a nutty taste and is often served as an accompaniment to strong-tasting meat, such as game. To cook wild rice, bring it to the boil in water, drain and cook in a little fresh water for about 30 minutes or until the grains are just beginning to open.

Ground Rice

Often used in shortbread or to make Asian milk desserts.

Rice Flour

Finer than ground rice, this is usually used in Asian dishes, but can be used as a thickener instead of cornflour.

Bran

This is the thin, papery, outer layer of the wheat grain. It is one of the best sources of dietary fibre and can be eaten for breakfast and used in place of a little of the flour in cakes, breads and biscuits.

Wheat Germ

The heart of the wheat grain, it should be stored in the fridge because the oil it contains quickly goes rancid. Sprinkle it on breakfast cereals, toast it and use it as a topping for steamed vegetables or include it in meat and nut loaves.

CORN (MAIZE)

Popping Corn

This is corn which has been allowed to dry. To make popcorn, put a tablespoon of oil in a heavy pan and when it is hot, add ½ cup popping corn. Cover the pan, shake from time to time and allow it to pop. When the popping stops, remove the pan from the heat and serve with melted butter and salt if you like. Be careful not to have the heat too high or the corn will burn.

Cornmeal

Used in the United States, especially the south, to make cornbread, Johnny cakes and hushpuppies. In Mexico and South America, a finer cornmeal is made into tortillas. In Italy cornmeal is used to make polenta. In this country we don't use cornmeal much, except occasionally, for baking.

Cornflour

This is the white heart of the corn kernel, ground very fine. It is usually used to thicken sauces and custards, and sometimes in biscuits and shortbread.

WHEAT
Wholewheat Grain

This is available in health food shops. Soak it overnight in water then simmer for 2 hours or until it is tender. Eat it in the same way as you would boiled rice, with meat, fish or vegetables. Or you can serve it for breakfast, as you would porridge.

Cracked or Kibbled Wheat

This is exactly the same as wholewheat except that is has been cracked between rollers. Its nutritional value is the same as wholewheat and it can be eaten in the same way, but it takes only about 20 minutes to cook.

Burghul or Bulgar

This is cracked wheat that has been hulled and parboiled. Burghul is most commonly used in tabouleh (taboolie), the Lebanese salad of parsley, onion, mint, burghul and tomatoes.

BARLEY

Pot or Scotch Barley

This is the whole grain, with only the outer husk removed. It can be bought in some health food shops and should be soaked overnight and cooked for several hours until tender.

Pearl Barley

This is the type most easily obtainable here. It is polished, like white rice, and doesn't need soaking. It takes about 1½ hours to cook. Use it in soup, with slow-cooked lamb dishes or as an accompaniment to meat or vegetables.

Rolled Barley

This is used to make porridge in the same way as rolled oats. It can also be used in muesli.

PULSES

The pulse family — beans, peas and lentils — is nature's recipe for a healthy balanced diet.

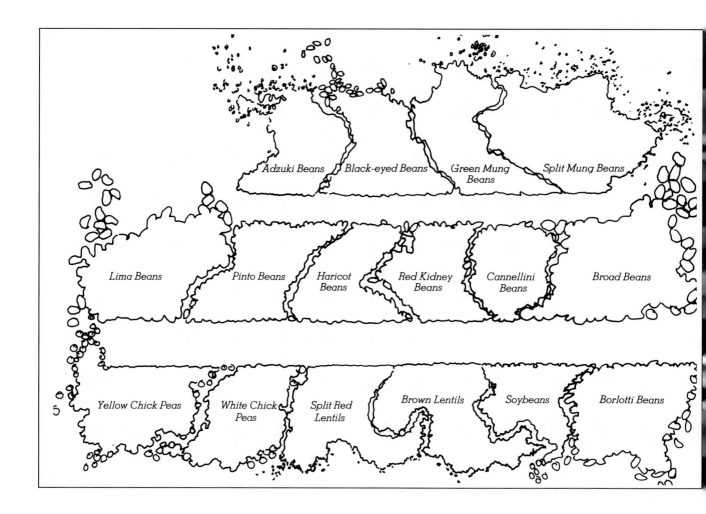

Adzuki Beans   *Black-eyed Beans*   *Green Mung Beans*   *Split Mung Beans*

Lima Beans   *Pinto Beans*   *Haricot Beans*   *Red Kidney Beans*   *Cannellini Beans*   *Broad Beans*

Yellow Chick Peas   *White Chick Peas*   *Split Red Lentils*   *Brown Lentils*   *Soybeans*   *Borlotti Beans*

PULSES

Pulses, which is the name given to dried beans and peas, are a good source of protein and dietary fibre. Years ago, split peas and lentils were the only pulses that we ate on a regular basis, usually in the form of soup. With the growing interest in Middle Eastern, Mexican and Indian food, pulses have become more popular and more readily available. Their biggest, and most well-known drawback is their tendency to produce flatulence.

When pulses are eaten with grains, along with a green vegetable, they provide a completely balanced diet. So-called primitive cultures, completely unaware of nutritional principles, have been eating like this for centuries.

Pulses will keep well for up to a year; if kept for longer than that, they will harden and become difficult to cook. Most pulses should be soaked in cold water before cooking, to clean and tenderise them. Discard any that are discoloured or that float to the surface when stirred. If you're in a hurry, you can put them into a pan of cold, unsalted water, bring them to the boil and simmer for 5 minutes. Cover the pan, remove it from the heat and allow the pulses to cool before cooking them.

They should not be cooked in salted water as the salt will encourage the skins to split and the insides will harden. If you want to add salt, do so towards the end of cooking.

Adzuki Beans

These are used to make flour for cakes and pastries in Japan. They are very sweet, and among the most easily digestible of all dried beans. They are small, reddish-brown beans with a cream ridge. They contain dietary fibre, protein and iron. Wash them thoroughly under running water, then soak in cold water for 2–3 hours before cooking. They should be simmered for 1½–2 hours by which time they should be tender enough to mash into a paste and use in Japanese and Chinese desserts.

Black-eyed Beans

Sometimes called black-eyed peas, these are small and kidney shaped, creamy in colour with a black splotch. They contain vitamin B1, dietary fibre, protein, iron and potassium.

After soaking they should be simmered for 1 hour. They may be used in soups and casseroles or as a salad, dressed with oil, garlic and lemon juice.

Borlotti Beans

Also called cranberry beans, these are large plump kidney-shaped beans, beige to brown and speckled with burgundy markings. They are a good source of vitamin B1 dietary fibre, iron, protein and potassium. They also supply calcium and some B vitamins.

After soaking they should be simmered for 1½–2 hours. They are used in Italian dishes, particularly stews and they are often mixed with rice.

Broad Beans

Most people cook with fresh broad beans, when they are green. When dried the colour ranges from olive green to brown. They have a high water content, so their nutrients are less concentrated. They contain vitamin C, and some dietary fibre and potassium.

They should be soaked, and the water changed before cooking. Simmer for 2½ hours. They are the basis of falafel, the Middle Eastern fried patties and for this dish they are not cooked, just soaked. Then they are pounded and flavoured with garlic, onions, cumin, coriander and parsley. They can also be used in soups, stews and bean salads.

Butter Beans

Similar in shape to broad beans, these are large, plump and white. They are a good source of protein, dietary fibre, potassium, vitamins B1 and B6.

After soaking they should be simmered for 2 hours until tender. Butter beans often become mushy when cooked and so they are best used in soups and purees.

Cannellini Beans

These are white kidney beans, larger than haricot beans, with squared-off ends. They are a good source of vitamins B1 and B2, protein, iron, dietary fibre and also contain calcium.

After soaking, simmer for 1½ hours. They are used in Italian dishes, particularly a salad made with tinned tuna and cannellini, tossed in a garlicky vinaigrette. They can also be used in soups and casseroles.

Chick Peas

There are two types available, the large white garbanzos and small, brown desi chick peas. The large ones do not need as long a soaking time as the small ones. However, even garbanzos often need a long soaking and cooking time to become tender. They contain dietary fibre, protein, iron, vitamin B1 and potassium.

After soaking, chick peas should be cooked gently for 2½ hours, sometimes longer, before they are tender. Skinned chick peas need less time — 1½–2 hours. They are pureed and used in hummus, the delicious Middle Eastern dip; in Israel they are used in falafel and in Greece they are roasted in the oven and served with drinks.

Haricot Beans

Small, white, oval beans, these are an excellent source of dietary fibre and a good source of protein, vitamin B1, potassium and iron.

They should be boiled, after soaking, for 1½ hours and used to make baked beans, or stews and casseroles. They are the main ingredient in the famous French regional dish, cassoulet. Haricot beans are often used for filling pastry cases when baking 'blind'.

Lentils

There are several types, the most commonly available are green (or brown) lentils, which can be soaked before cooking, although it's not strictly necessary, and split red lentils, which don't need to be soaked and which become tender after 20–30 minutes cooking.

Lentils are a good source of dietary fibre, protein, iron, potassium and vitamins B1, B2, B6. Wash them thoroughly before cooking. Red lentils are cooked for 30 minutes, green or brown lentils will take 1–1½ hours. Use lentils to make soups, purees and dhal.

Lima Beans

These are very similar to butter beans and can be substituted for them. They come in two sizes, small and large. The small beans are either green or white, the large beans are white. They contain vitamin C, dietary fibre, protein, iron and some B vitamins.

After soaking, simmer for 1½ hours and use in salads and stews.

Mung Beans

The most common type of mung bean is the green one, but black mung beans are also available as are split mung beans. They contain dietary fibre, protein, iron and B vitamins.

They can be cooked (there's no need to soak them), but they have a tendency to become rather sticky. They are usually sprouted and used in salads and stir-fry dishes.

Pinto Beans

These are similar in appearance to borlotti beans, beige coloured with brown specks. They contain vitamin B1, iron, protein, potassium, dietary fibre and some calcium.

After soaking, simmer them for 1–1½ hours and use in stews, chilli con carne, and other meat and bean dishes.

Red Kidney Beans

Dark red, kidney-shaped beans, they contain dietary fibre, protein, iron, potassium and several B vitamins.

They should be soaked and then simmered for 1½ hours and fried with onions and chilli as a filling for tacos, or they can be used in soups and casseroles.

Soybeans

These are small, very hard beige-coloured oval beans. They are the most nutritious of all beans, containing vitamin B1, protein, iron, dietary fibre and calcium. The Chinese, who have been using soybeans, and soybean products for thousands of years, call them 'the meat of the earth'.

They take a very long time to become tender. After soaking, cover them with fresh water and simmer for 3½–4 hours. They can be used to make very nutritious baked beans, or in any dish that requires red kidney beans or haricot beans, increasing the cooking times accordingly.

Split Peas

These are probably the most well-known pulses. Everyone at some time has had pea and ham soup. There are two types available, green and yellow. They are a good source of vitamin B1, protein, iron, pantothenic acid, potassium, dietary fibre and some B vitamins.

They don't need to be soaked. They should be covered with plenty of cold water and simmered for 1½ hours without stirring (stirring will encourage them to stick to the pan). Use in soups and pureed, as a vegetable.

Whole Dried Peas

Also called blue peas or Dun peas, these are blue-green or brown, round, dimpled and hard dry peas. Blue peas produce green split peas, brown peas produce yellow split peas. They contain vitamin B1, protein, potassium, dietary fibre, iron, pantothenic acid and other B vitamins.

They should be soaked overnight and cooked in fresh water for 1 hour. They break up during cooking so should be used in soups or as a puree.

VEGETABLES

The variety and flavour of versatile vegetables. Great with every meal or on their own.

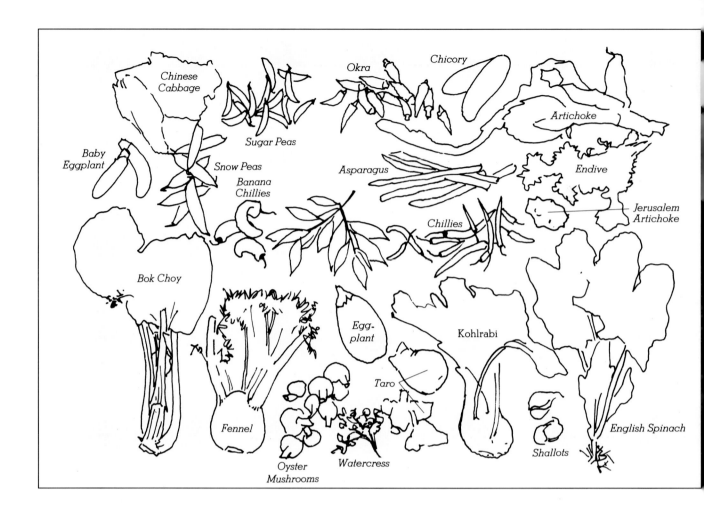

VEGETABLES

Asparagus

The asparagus season is short so make the most of it. When buying asparagus, look for firm stalks with no wrinkling. The tips should be tightly furled and shouldn't wilt. Wash them well before cooking. Thin asparagus doesn't need to be peeled, but thick asparagus should have its stalks peeled before cooking, because it can be a bit woody.

Cut a slice off the base of the stalks and tie them in bundles. If you have a mixture of thick and thin stalks, cook the thick stalks first, and add the thin stalks later, since they don't take as long to cook. Stand them upright in an asparagus steamer or in a saucepan with boiling water to come about a third of the way up the stems. Cover with foil, or an upturned saucepan of the same diameter, so that the stalks will boil and the tips will steam.

The most common mistake in cooking asparagus is to overcook it. Test thin asparagus after 5 minutes, thick asparagus after 8 minutes, you should be able to pierce the stem with a skewer, but it should still be firm. Asparagus may be eaten with the fingers and is usually served hot with melted butter or hollandaise sauce and cold with vinaigrette.

Artichokes

Twist or cut the stalk level with the base, then cut the base flush so that it will sit up straight on a plate. Cut off about ¼ of the top of the artichoke, wash it and boil in water acidulated with lemon juice. Alternatively you can tie a slice of lemon to each artichoke. This prevents it from browning. Test by pulling away one of the leaves. When it comes off easily, the artichoke is cooked.

To eat a whole artichoke, pull off the leaves, one at a time, and dip into melted butter or hollandaise sauce, then draw it through your teeth, eating only the fleshy part at the bottom of the leaf and discarding the rest. Cold artichokes can be dipped into vinaigrette.

When you come to the centre of the artichoke, you'll find a little cone of light-coloured leaves. Pull these off and scrape out the hairy choke with a teaspoon. The heart of the artichoke, which is considered the best part, can be eaten with a knife and fork.

Jerusalem Artichokes

These are not in any way similar to globe artichokes, but are small knobby tubers. Scrub them and peel off their thin skin, but use them immediately as their flesh turns a greyish-purple when exposed to the air. Boil them in water acidulated with lemon juice to prevent this. Once boiled they may be sauteed in oil or butter until golden brown.

Shallots

What is known in Australia as shallots, and in America as scallions, the rest of the English speaking world calls spring onions. Real shallots grow in little bulbs just like garlic, but have a red, papery skin, similar in colour and texture to Spanish onions.

Although not as pungent as ordinary brown onions, they have a more intense flavour, suitable for using in subtly-flavoured sauces, such as beurre blanc. The shallots used in the recipes in this book refer to spring onions.

Chicory (Whitloof)

Sometimes called Belgian endive, this is often used raw as a salad, sliced diagonally and dressed with oil and lemon juice. Or the leaves can be separated and it can be mixed with other salad greens. Chicory is also good braised in butter, but it is slightly bitter when cooked, so first blanch it in water acidulated with a little lemon juice, then drain and braise.

Eggplant (Aubergine)

Most of the eggplants we see are big ones, either bulbous or long and slim. These need to be salted before cooking, to eliminate their bitter juices. Cut them in half or slice them, depending upon what dish you're going to use them for, and sprinkle salt over them. Don't peel them. Put them in a colander, rest a weighted plate on top and leave them for 30 minutes. Rinse well and dry with paper towels. Baby eggplants usually don't require salting. If you're frying eggplants, use good quality olive oil for the most delicious combination of flavours.

Endive

A salad vegetable with curly leaves, this is sometimes known as chicory in Australia. Make it into a salad in exactly the same way you would a lettuce, i.e. wash it and drain it well. Because endive is more bitter than lettuce, it needs a strongly-flavoured dressing, perhaps made with mustard or blue cheese, and it goes well with such additions as crumbled grilled bacon, anchovies and olives.

English Spinach

What's known in New South Wales as spinach is known everywhere else as silverbeet. What's known in New South Wales as English spinach, is known everywhere else as simply, spinach. It has a much more delicate taste than silverbeet and is delicious raw in a salad. However it wilts very quickly and must be bought and used when it's very fresh.

The small stems are removed and so are the midribs from each leaf, if they are coarse. This is done by folding the spinach leaf inwards and pulling the stalk up towards the tip.

Then it is prepared in the same way as silverbeet. It is washed very thoroughly and, if you are cooking it, it is cooked in just the water that clings to it. When wilted, it is drained thoroughly, chopped finely and mixed with pepper, a little freshly grated nutmeg, some butter or cream.

Watercress

This is becoming more popular in Australia now, and more readily available. If not using immediately, store it standing in a bowl of water in the fridge. Always wash thoroughly before using.

Watercress make delicious soups, sauces and sandwiches, it is also used as a garnish. The most boring thing about watercress is that to use it in any edible form, that is, not simply as a garnish, the leaves must be pulled off the stems. This can take some time. It has a slightly peppery taste and is an excellent addition to a green salad that would otherwise be bland.

Chinese Cabbage

This is used in the same way as you would ordinary cabbage, but it is most often used in Chinese dishes. It is delicious braised with oyster sauce. Not to be confused with bok choy.

Bok Choy

This grows in bunches with white fleshy stems and olive green leaves. You can buy it in most Asian stores that sell fresh vegetables, and it is now becoming more readily available at traditional greengrocers.

The tough stalk ends are discarded, but the stalks themselves are sliced and used with the leaves. It is mostly used in Chinese stir-fry recipes. Do not overcook, or the texture will be ruined.

Kohlrabi

The edible part of the kohlrabi is its bulbous stem. It has shoots growing out of the bulb, which should be cut off when preparing it for cooking. Choose the smallest kohlrabi you can find — the vegetable becomes coarse and fibrous as it grows larger. Peel them, cut off the shoots and cook them whole or sliced in boiling water. They can then be sliced into julienne strips, tossed in vinaigrette and eaten as a salad, or sauteed in butter for a few minutes. Kohlrabi has a delicate cabbage taste.

Oyster Mushrooms

These are now much more readily available than they used to be. They can be eaten raw or cooked in the same way as button or field mushrooms. They should be clean and pale in colour, with no sign of sliminess.

Snow Peas

Snow peas (also called mangetout) need to be topped, tailed and strung. To do this, break off the tip at one end and pull it downwards, removing the string as you go. Break off the tip at the other end, and pull it upwards, taking off the string on the other side. If boiled or steamed whole for a few minutes only, they should remain crisp. Snow peas can be cut into julienne strips and blanched for 1–2 minutes, then refreshed in cold water, drained and added to salads.

Chillies

Green chillies are hotter than red chillies. If you want the taste of chillies in a dish, but not the searing hotness, remove the seeds. To do this, chop off the stem end, slit the chilli down the middle and remove the seeds. Always wear rubber gloves to do this. If you don't and you touch your face or eyes, it will burn.

Banana Chillies

Sometimes called Hungarian chillies, these are much milder than green or red chillies. They give the flavour of chilli without its searing hotness.

Fennel

Fennel tastes of anise, and is either loved or hated. Buy it as fresh as possible. It should be white with a greenish tinge and the feathery leaves on top should look fresh. Any sign of yellowness is a sign of age. Fennel can be chopped and eaten as a salad with vinaigrette, added to a mixed salad or braised in butter or oil.

The leaves should be cut off, and the base should be trimmed. Then the fennel can be cut across into rings or vertically into leaves.

Sugar Peas (Snap Peas)

These have only been available for a few years and are quickly becoming popular. They are very sweet and all the pea is eaten, including the pods, just like snow peas. They should be topped and tailed and cooked quickly in salted water. They can be eaten cold in salads or hot, just as you would ordinary peas.

Okra

An acquired taste, okra have a viscous texture which gives body to the stews they are often included in. Creole and Cajun gumbos are the most famous dishes to include okra. Look for crisp pods, discarding any that are shrivelled. To cook them, trim off the tip and the cap, but make sure you don't expose the seeds or the okra will split during cooking and lose its shape. Cook in boiling salted water until tender.

Taro

In the photograph we have shown two types of taro which are available. They are not often seen in shops, but are becoming more popular and can be treated in much the same way as potatoes. They should be peeled, then boiled and mashed, or baked or sauteed. When boiled, the flesh will turn a greyish-green colour.

FRUITS

For snacks, starters and great endings, delicious, nutritious fruit is the answer.

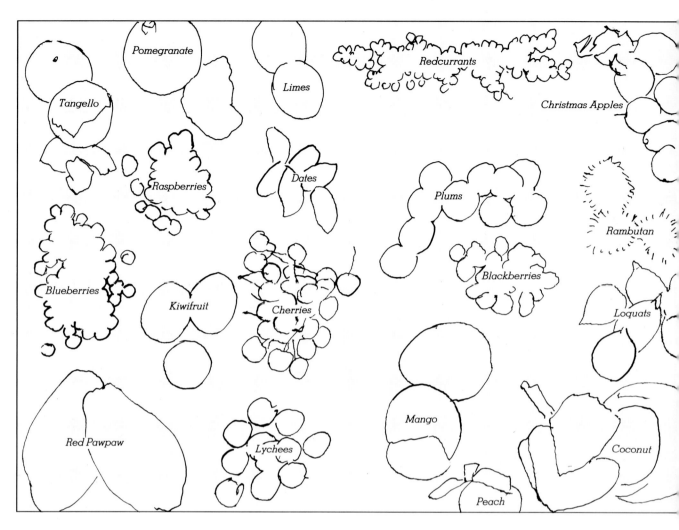

FRUITS

A platter piled high with fresh fruits is undoubtedly one of the most refreshing, delicious and simple ways to end a meal.

With people becoming more and more health conscious, fruit is a definite asset in this food revolution of changing eating patterns. Most of the desserts in this book consist of fresh, as well as some dried, fruits prepared and presented in interesting ways.

Full of minerals and vitamins, fresh fruit is great for snacks and as the base for entrees, soups, main meals plus the more traditional use of it in jams, chutneys and drinks. Its versatility extends beyond use in cooking though. Contents scooped out of fruits such as grapefruit, rockmelon, large oranges, pineapple and avocado leave fruit shells which make novel serving dishes. Pawpaw leaves wrapped around meat or octopus overnight, or pawpaw juice poured over meats is an ideal natural tenderiser.

Blueberry

Cultivation of blueberries is becoming more and more popular in Australia. The little black or dull blue coloured fruits grow in clusters on shrubs. They are used in muffins, pancakes, pies, cakes and biscuits, in sauces and stewed either alone or with apples, pears and quince. Blueberries go very well with spices such as cinnamon, coriander, ginger, nutmeg and cardamom. Serve fresh with sour cream or cottage cheese and brown sugar.

Raspberries

Raspberries are one of the sweetest and most delectable of berries. Raspberries can be eaten fresh, or served in compotes, cakes, flans, tarts, pancakes, jams or jellies. Raspberries pureed with cream are a tasty dressing for fruit desserts.

Tangello

Juicy and good for eating or use in salads, the tangello is a hybrid fruit; that is, a cross between a mandarin and a grapefruit. This fruit easily breaks into segments.

Avocado

Highly nutritional and easy to digest, avocados are available from April to December. There are over 70 different varieties with the three most popular ones being: the pear-shaped Sharwil variety with a smooth green skin; the pebbled, green skinned Fuerte; or the slightly smaller Hass with a purplish-black skin. They are soft but firm when ripe. Avocado is the basis of the delicious Mexican dip, Guacamole. Sliced avocado is popular in salads and pureed avocado combined with other ingredients makes tasty sauces. Lemon juice sprinkled over avocado slices prevents browning. If cooking with avocado, its delicate, subtle flavours can easily be destroyed if overheated.

Babaco

These have just started coming onto the market. They originated in Ecuador, but now are grown in New Zealand. They are a relative of the pawpaw but are not as sweet. Their taste has been described as a blend of pineapple and pawpaw with a hint of strawberry. Babaco is often sold when it is green, but it must not be eaten until it ripens and turns yellow.

Blackberry

Blackberries are very nourishing, containing a high proportion of calcium, vitamin B1 plus other vitamins and minerals. The fruit is first green and as it ripens turns red and then a deep black. Blackberries can be served fresh or else in jams, tarts, etc. Because of their 'pippy' texture, a lot of blackberry cooking requires straining the pulp and using the extracted juice.

Lychees

When ripe, the skin of the lychee should be red. They taste best when they're slightly chilled. Peel them and eat them just as they are, removing the glossy stone in the centre. You can also serve them, peeled and stoned, mixed with strawberries or other fruit.

Mangoes

Avoid buying mangoes with black marks on the skin, they indicate that rot might be present. Mangoes are extremely messy to eat; most experts agree that to eat a mango whole, one should do it in the bath. To serve a mango elegantly, cut it down both sides of the seed, to give two fat 'cheeks'. Score the mango flesh diagonally with a sharp knife, then turn and score it diagonally the other way, to make a diamond pattern. Make sure you don't cut right through to the skin. Holding the mango at both corners, turn it outwards so that the little diamonds pop up. Serve with a spoon and fork. That leaves you with the mango stone and all the flesh adhering to it. You have little choice but to suck it over the kitchen sink.

Rambutan

Treatment of this odd looking fruit is very similar to that of lychees — peel it, eat the flesh and discard the seed. The flesh can be eaten fresh, used in salads, canned, preserved or bottled. Originating from Malaysia, rambutan flesh is white to grey and adheres to a flattened seed.

Redcurrant

These small, brightly coloured currants are closely related to the blackcurrant. An offshoot of the redcurrant is the whitecurrant — both of which grow on shrubs. Unripe currants can be used in cooking, and although they do not require as much sweetening as may be expected, they go well with honey. Redcurrants can be combined with blackcurrants, raspberries, strawberries, loganberries and cherries in a delicious jam. Redcurrants can be crystallised or frosted by dipping in egg white and then dusting with caster sugar and leaving to dry. In little bunches, these make an attractive decoration.

Pomegranates

The larger the fruit the better the flavour. They should be crimson, brownish red or bright red. Cut through the skin all the way around, then break them open. The seeds can be sucked of flesh and then discarded, or they can be eaten. The flesh around the seeds however, is regarded as the edible part. The white pith is bitter and should not be eaten.

Tamarillos

When ripe, tamarillos should be firm but not hard. They can be cut in half and eaten with a spoon, but if you are cooking them, the skin must be removed as it is bitter. Pour boiling water over them, leave for 2 minutes, after which the skin will peel off, just like a tomato. They make a delicious sauce for smoked meats, pork and lamb.

Pawpaws

When buying pawpaws, avoid any with shrivelled skin or bruises. The fragrance is a good indicator of ripeness. Cut into wedges, remove the seeds, squeeze lime juice over them, and eat chilled for breakfast. Pawpaws can also be added to fruit salads or made into a sorbet. Pawpaw is a natural meat tenderiser so you can mix it with meat for an hour or so before you cook it, to make it more succulent.

Kiwifruit

This fruit with its hairy, egg-shaped appearance originally came from China, hence its name — Chinese gooseberry. However, in New Zealand it was grown on such a viable commercial scale that nowadays few people know this fruit by its original name. The kiwifruit has a green flesh and a mass of tiny black seeds. The flesh is ideal for use in ice creams and sorbets and surprisingly, is also a good meat tenderiser. The colour of the kiwifruit also makes it a very attractive decoration for fruit dishes and desserts.

Coconut

Coconut cream with its creamy, thick base is an exquisite addition to curries, adding texture and flavour. Coconut cream is easily made by pureeing 2 cups of water with 1 cup of grated coconut and then straining the puree. To collect the milk of a coconut without having it splattered everywhere, pierce two of the eyes and pour the milk out. Then split the shell open with a hammer. The white meat can be grated in a blender and one coconut produces about 4 cups of grated coconut.

Loquat

Ginger, lemon juice and crystallised fruit go well with loquats. They can be eaten fresh and also used in fruit compotes, made into jams, and preserved. Loquats with their yellow to yellow-orange skin, are available in spring and early summer.

Carob

Growing in pods up to 30 cm long, carob is used as an alternative to cocoa. It is very sweet with a sugar content as high as 50 per cent. However, many people still prefer carob combined with a sweetener; an ideal mix is honey. Before using the carob pod, the hard seeds must be removed from the pod.

Cumquat

Similar in appearance to a very small mandarin, the cumquat ripens at the end of summer with the fruit changing from a green to vivid orange colour. Cumquats are usually not eaten raw, the Australian varieties tend to be too sour. However, there are some varieties available which add a bite to rice dishes and green salads. Jams and chutneys is the usual preparation for this fruit. A true delicacy is cumquats left to soak in a sugar syrup and brandy for a few months. The brandied fruit can then be used in desserts and the brandy, as a delightful drink.

Date

We are all familiar with the dried dates, but now fresh dates are becoming more and more available in fruit shops. The very sweet flavour of dates lends this fruit to being used in cakes and desserts. Dates make an interesting addition to rice dishes and curries and are a delicious accompaniment to spiced and cold meats. More exotic preparations include stoned dates stuffed with fondant, nuts, especially almonds, crystallised fruits or marzipan.

Fig

Figs, usually pear-shaped, vary in colours from white or green to red-purple and black. Fresh figs need not be peeled before being eaten, unless the skin is very thick. Dried figs are considerably sweeter with the sugar content increasing by over 30 per cent. In Italy and Greece fresh figs are served as an antipasto with slices of meat such as prosciutto or on its own with freshly ground black pepper. Ginger, cream, nuts, cinnamon and citrus fruits all go well with figs. Liqueurs are another interesting addition to this sugary, syrupy, uniquely flavoured fruit.

≡SOUPS≡

Soups don't have to be served before the main course, they can be the main course. A big bowl of minestrone, sprinkled with Parmesan, eaten with crusty bread and followed by a salad, is a balanced, nutritious and sustaining meal. Lighter soups, such as cream of vegetable soups, can also be the main part of a meal, but since they are much less sustaining and nutritious, they should be accompanied by a sandwich or a mixed salad.

Most soups require stock as their basis. Stock cubes can be used but be aware of how much salt is in them. If you don't make your own chicken stock, enquire at your local take away chicken shop as some of them now sell frozen chicken stock; or use vegetable stock, made by keeping the water in which you've cooked your vegetables.

Making soup is much easier than it once was if you have a blender or food processor. Be careful though that you don't put too much liquid in it or it will drip down the sides and all over your kitchen bench. It's better to remove the vegetables from the saucepan with a slotted spoon and add just a little of the stock to the food processor before you puree.

BEAN AND PEA SOUP

¼ cup red kidney beans
¼ cup lima beans
¼ cup yellow split peas
¼ cup chick peas
freshly ground black pepper
2 tablespoons oil
½ cup chopped onions
½ cup chopped red capsicum
¼ cup chopped celery
¼ cup chopped carrots
1 tablespoon chopped fresh parsley
1 clove garlic, chopped
4 cups stock (chicken, vegetable or beef)
1 bay leaf
pinch dried marjoram
pinch dried basil
½ cup chopped peeled tomatoes

Soak beans and peas overnight in water to cover. Next day, cook in the water until they are tender and discard the liquid. The chick peas will take longer to cook than the other pulses.

Heat the oil in a large saucepan and add the onion, capsicum, celery, carrot, parsley and garlic. Cook, stirring for 5 minutes or until the onion is soft. Add the stock and simmer until the vegetables are tender.

Add the beans and peas and all the remaining ingredients and simmer for 20 minutes. Remove the bay leaf before serving.
Serves 4

GAZPACHO ON ICE

6 cloves garlic
1 tablespoon sugar
2 tablespoons paprika
6 tablespoons olive oil
2 tablespoons wine vinegar
pinch cayenne pepper
400 g canned tomatoes
4 cups chicken stock
1 cucumber, peeled and diced
24 shallots, finely sliced
1-2 green capsicums, cut into tiny cubes

Put the garlic, sugar, paprika, oil, vinegar and cayenne pepper into a blender and puree. Add the tomatoes and blend again.

Combine the blended ingredients and the stock in a large bowl. Add the diced cucumber to the soup and cover with plastic. Chill.

To serve, pour the soup over ice cubes in individual bowls and sprinkle with chopped shallots and capsicum.
Serves 8

Gazpacho On Ice (above) and Cold Yoghurt and Cucumber Soup

CREAMED OYSTER SOUP

4 dozen oysters, removed from the shell
500 mL milk
500 mL cream
½ teaspoon celery seeds
1 tablespoon finely chopped celery leaves
freshly ground black pepper
dash Worcestershire sauce
pinch cayenne pepper

Mix the oysters with the milk and cream. Add celery seeds and leaves, pepper and Worcestershire sauce. Bring almost to the boil, dust with cayenne pepper and serve.
Serves 4-6

COLD YOGHURT AND CUCUMBER SOUP

1 cucumber, peeled and diced
2 cups chicken stock
2 cloves garlic, crushed
500 mL natural yoghurt
juice ½ lemon
pinch dried coriander
1 cup iced water
4-6 very thin lemon slices (optional)
2 tablespoons chopped walnuts (optional)

Put cucumber and stock in a saucepan and simmer until the cucumber is just tender. Chill until required.

Combine the garlic, yoghurt, lemon juice and coriander. Stir into the chilled soup with iced water. Serve topped with lemon slices and sprinkled with chopped walnuts.
Serves 4-6

CHINESE GREEN SOUP

1 tablespoon oil
½ teaspoon grated ginger root
1 clove garlic, crushed
5 cups hot chicken or vegetable stock
1 cup rice
750 g Chinese cabbage, finely shredded
6 shallots, finely chopped
1 tablespoon dry sherry
½ teaspoon sesame oil

Heat the oil in a saucepan and saute the ginger and garlic for 1 minute. Pour in the hot stock and add the rice. Simmer for 15 minutes or until the rice is just tender. Add the cabbage and shallots and simmer for 5 minutes. Stir in the sherry and sesame oil and serve.
Serves 4-6

SPICY CHICKEN AND AVOCADO SOUP

6 cups chicken stock
1 chicken breast
2 onions, thinly sliced
½ teaspoon dried coriander
½ teaspoon dried oregano
1 teaspoon curry powder
freshly ground black pepper
1 large avocado

Put the chicken stock into a saucepan with the chicken breast, onions and seasonings. Bring to the boil and simmer for 15 minutes. Remove chicken, strain the stock and discard the onion. Remove the skin from the chicken and slice the meat into thin strips. Return it to the stock, heat, but do not allow it to boil.

Peel the avocado and slice thinly. Place slices in individual soup bowls and pour the soup over. The slices will float on top. Serve immediately before the avocado begins to brown.
Serves 6

LEMON SOUP

1 egg yolk
2 tablespoons lemon juice
440 g can chicken consomme
225 mL water
4 tablespoons cooked rice
2 tablespoons finely chopped fresh parsley

Beat the egg yolk with lemon juice. Heat the soup with water and add rice. Slowly add a little hot soup to the egg-lemon mixture and then pour it back into the soup. Season to taste and decorate with chopped parsley.
Serves 4

ICED BUTTERMILK SOUP

1 small cucumber
salt
3 cups stock (chicken or vegetable)
3 cups buttermilk
1 teaspoon prepared French mustard
2 tablespoons minced celery
2 teaspoons chopped chives
2 teaspoons chopped fresh dill
2 teaspoons chopped fresh parsley

Peel and finely dice the cucumber. Place it in a colander, sprinkle with salt and allow to stand for 30 minutes. Rinse the cucumber in cold water to remove excess salt and dry on paper towels.

Place the cucumber in a large bowl, add all the remaining ingredients and mix well. Chill before serving.
Serves 4-6

CHILLED PUMPKIN SOUP

1 kg pumpkin, peeled and diced
4 cups chicken stock
1 onion, chopped
4 shallots, sliced
¼ cup cream
freshly ground black pepper
chives, to garnish

Cook pumpkin in water until tender. Drain, cool and puree in a blender or food processor. Cook the stock with onion and shallots for 15 minutes, cool and strain.

Mix the pumpkin into the stock, season to taste, serve with a swirl of cream, cover and chill. Garnish with chives.
Serves 6

COUNTRY HARVEST SOUP

60 g wholewheat grain
50 g butter
1 small onion, finely chopped
115 g walnuts
1½ cups chicken or vegetable stock
1 bouquet garni
1 tablespoon flour
¼ teaspoon dry mustard
2 cups milk
125 g Cheddar cheese, grated
2 tablespoons cream (optional)

Soak the wheat in boiling water for 1 hour. Melt half the butter in a large saucepan and saute the onion until it is soft but not brown. Grind the walnuts on a board with a rolling pin. Drain the wheat and add it to the pan with the walnuts, stock and bouquet garni. Bring to the boil, cover and simmer for about 1 hour, or until the wheat is tender.

Melt the remaining butter in a separate pan, stir in the flour and mustard and cook for 2 minutes, stirring continuously. Remove the pan from the heat and gradually add the milk, stirring continuously. Slowly bring to the boil and simmer for 3 minutes, still stirring.

Add the sauce to the wheat mixture with the grated cheese and season to taste. Heat gently, without boiling and stir in the cream if used.
Serves 6

Chilled Pumpkin Soup

CARROT AND ORANGE SOUP

750 g carrots, sliced
1 onion, chopped
2 sticks celery, chopped
4 cups chicken or vegetable stock
1 bay leaf
1 tablespoon cornflour
grated rind and juice 1 orange
pinch nutmeg
freshly ground black pepper
¼ cup cream
bay leaves, to garnish

Place the vegetables in a pan with the stock and bay leaf. Cover and simmer for 20 minutes until the vegetables are tender. Puree the vegetables in a blender or through a sieve. Blend the cornflour with a little of the stock and return it to the saucepan with the pureed vegetables, orange rind and juice and nutmeg. Season to taste.

Bring to the boil and simmer for 3 minutes, stirring. Pour soup into a serving bowl and decorate with a swirl of cream. Garnish with bay leaves.
Serves 4-6

PEA AND BARLEY SOUP

½ cup barley
2 cups water
4 cups stock (chicken, vegetable or beef)
20 g butter
1 tablespoon flour
freshly ground black pepper
½ cup milk
1 carrot, peeled and cut in strips
1 cup green peas
1 tablespoon chopped chives, to garnish

Soak the barley in the water overnight. Drain, rinse and place in a saucepan with the stock. Cover and simmer for 1 hour or until the barley is tender. Strain, reserving 4 tablespoons of the cooked barley. Use the rest of the barley for another dish.

Melt the butter and stir in the flour and pepper. Cook for 1 minute, then add the strained stock and bring to the boil, stirring constantly.

Add the milk and reserved barley and simmer while you prepare the vegetables.

Cook the carrot with the peas in water until just tender. Drain and add to the soup. Serve garnished with chives.
Serves 4

Clockwise from top: Cream of Choko Soup, Fresh Tomato Soup and Carrot and Orange Soup

LENTIL SOUP

250 g brown lentils
1 onion, finely chopped
1 clove garlic, crushed
2 tablespoons parsley, finely chopped
2 tablespoons oil
2 large tomatoes, peeled and seeded
2 tablespoons white wine vinegar (optional)

Soak the lentils in water for 1 hour. Simmer in the same water for 1 hour. Saute the onion, garlic and parsley in the oil until the onion is soft but not brown. Add the tomatoes and cook for 5 minutes.

Combine the tomato mixture with the lentils and reheat before serving. Add vinegar if using. It gives a pleasantly sharp taste to the soup.
Serves 4-6

ICED CLODNICK

450 g canned sliced beetroot
1 cup sour cream
2 cups cold white wine
1 cucumber, peeled and diced
125 g cooked peeled prawns
freshly ground black pepper
2 tablespoons finely chopped fresh dill

In a large bowl, whisk together the juice from the beetroot, the sour cream and wine. Dice the beetroot and add to the liquid with the cucumber. Add the prawns and season to taste.

Cover with plastic wrap and chill until needed. To serve, pour over ice cubes in individual bowls and sprinkle with dill.
Serves 4-6

CREAM OF CHOKO SOUP

6 chokos
1 onion, chopped
1 stick celery, chopped
½ cup rice
6 cups stock (chicken or vegetable)
freshly ground black pepper
1 clove garlic, crushed
½ cup sour cream (optional)
capsicum, cut in strips

Peel the chokos, remove the hard core and chop roughly. Place chokos, onion, celery, rice, stock, pepper and garlic in a saucepan and simmer for 45 minutes.

Cool and puree the soup in a blender or through a sieve. Return it to the saucepan and stir in the sour cream over low heat. Do not allow it to boil. Serve hot with a dollop of sour cream if desired. Garnish with capsicum strips.
Serves 4-6

FRESH TOMATO SOUP

25 g butter
1 onion, thinly sliced
1 carrot, thinly sliced
1 tablespoon flour
750 g tomatoes, peeled and quartered
3 cups chicken or vegetable stock
1 bay leaf
pinch ground mace
freshly ground black pepper
fresh rosemary, to garnish

Melt the butter in a large pan, add the onion and carrot, cover and cook over low heat for 8 minutes. Remove the pan from the heat and stir in the flour.

Add the tomatoes, stock, bay leaf, mace and season to taste. Bring to the boil, cover and simmer for 20-30 minutes. Puree the soup in a blender or through a sieve and return to the rinsed-out pan. Reheat before serving. Garnish with rosemary.
Serves 6

WATERCRESS AND VERMICELLI SOUP

75 g watercress
2 onions, sliced
1 litre chicken stock
75 g vermicelli

Wash the watercress thoroughly and discard the stalks. Place the watercress, onion and stock in a pan and simmer for 15 minutes. Add the vermicelli and simmer for 2 minutes or until tender. Pour into a serving dish.
Serves 4-6

CHILLED GREEN PEA SOUP

2 cups frozen peas
4 lettuce leaves, shredded
1 cup chopped shallots
1 cup water
2 cups chicken stock
4 tablespoons sour cream or yoghurt
1 tablespoon chopped fresh mint

Bring peas, lettuce and shallots to the boil in the water. Lower the heat, cover and simmer for 8 minutes. Puree in a blender or food processor.

Transfer to a bowl and blend in the chicken stock. Cover and chill until required. To serve, stir in the sour cream or yoghurt and decorate with mint.
Serves 4-6

Minestrone

ICED ORANGE AND TOMATO SOUP

350 mL can tomato juice, well chilled
250 mL freshly squeezed orange juice
1 tablespoon grated orange rind
250 mL cream
Freshly ground black pepper
1 avocado
Lemon juice

Place the tomato juice, orange juice, orange rind and cream in a blender and mix well. Season to taste.

Peel the avocado, remove the stone and slice the flesh thinly. Pour over a little lemon juice to prevent it from browning.

Serve the soup over ice cubes and avocado slices in individual bowls.
Serves 4–6

Clockwise from top: Chilled Green Pea Soup, Iced Orange and Tomato Soup and Iced Beetroot Soup

ICED BEETROOT SOUP

1 litre water
2 cloves garlic
½ bunch celery, finely chopped
1 small onion, chopped
2 tomatoes, peeled and chopped
450 g canned beetroot
2 tablespoons red wine vinegar
2 tablespoons sugar
3 tablespoons lemon juice
3 egg yolks, beaten
300 mL sour cream
snipped chives, to garnish

Place the water in a saucepan with garlic, celery, onion, tomatoes, beetroot, vinegar and sugar. Bring to the boil then lower the heat and simmer for 15 minutes. Remove from the heat, cool slightly, then pour into a blender or food processor and puree. (You may have to do this in 2 batches.) Strain soup.

Return the soup to the saucepan, place over very low heat, stir in the lemon juice and egg yolks until the soup is slightly thickened. Do not allow it to boil.

Cool, then cover and chill until required. To serve, stir in sour cream until well blended and sprinkle with chives.
Serves 6

MINESTRONE

⅓ cup cannellini or any small white beans
⅓ cup whole dried peas
9 cups chicken or vegetable stock
1 large stick celery, chopped
1 large onion, sliced
2 medium carrots, sliced
2 tomatoes, peeled and quartered
½ cup any leafy green vegetable, sliced
½ teaspoon dried basil
½ teaspoon dried oregano
½ cup macaroni
⅓ cup grated Parmesan cheese
chopped parsley to garnish

Soak the beans and peas together overnight in 3 cups of stock. The beans should be white and plump, the peas green and plump. Discard any that are hard, brown or wrinkled.

Add the peas, beans and their soaking stock to the remaining stock with the celery, onion and carrots in a large pan. Bring to the boil and simmer for 1–2 hours or until the beans and peas are tender. Add the tomatoes, leafy vegetable, basil and oregano. Cook for 10 minutes.

Add macaroni and cook for 10–15 minutes until it is tender. Serve with grated cheese and garnish with parsley.
Serves 6

FIRST COURSES

Most of the recipes in this chapter can double up as main courses for a light meal. Or you can serve them with other first courses or salads to make a one course meal consisting of several different things, very much in the Asian style.

This way of eating is starting to make sense to many cooks. Firstly, it's more casual than the traditional two or three course meals, and secondly, it's less work and strain for the cook. If everything is placed on the table at the same time the cook can sit down and eat with everyone else and not have to worry again until it's time for fruit or dessert.

Some of the dishes in this chapter however, such as Brains in Black Butter, should be eaten by themselves, with no accompaniment whatever.

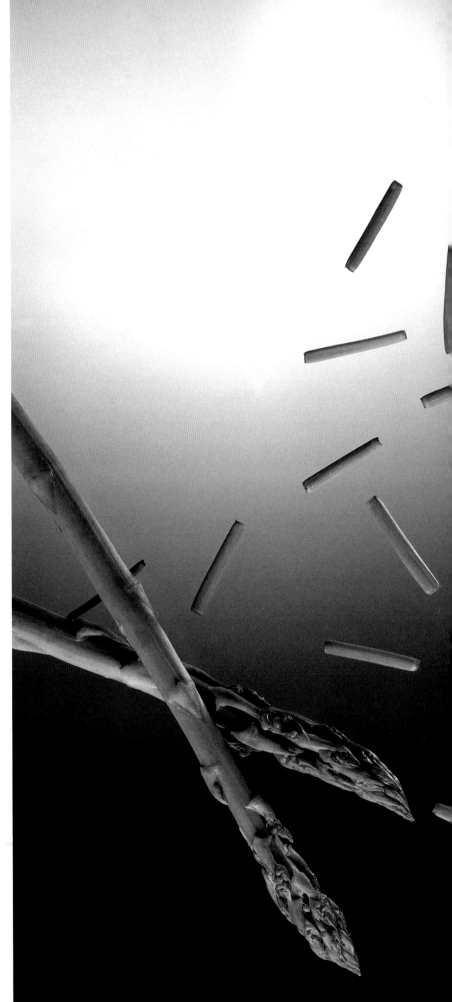

VEGETABLE PATE

1 leek, well washed
2 cups shelled peas
4 cups shredded spinach
1 egg
½ teaspoon dried tarragon
¼ teaspoon nutmeg
3 cups sliced carrots
freshly ground black pepper
60 g butter
½ cup water
2 tablespoons flour

Slice the white part of the leek into thin rounds and steam until tender. Line a loaf tin with oiled greaseproof paper and place the cooked leek on top, smoothing it down to make a thin layer.

Cook the peas in boiling water and steam the spinach over them. When the peas are tender, drain them and combine with the spinach, egg, tarragon and nutmeg in a blender or food processor and puree. Spoon the spinach/pea mixture over the leeks and smooth out the top with a spatula.

Cook the carrots with pepper, butter and water until they are tender. Drain off any remaining liquid and puree the carrots with the flour. Spoon the carrot puree over the spinach in the loaf tin and smooth the top with a spatula. Rap the tin on a bench to remove any air bubbles.

Place greaseproof paper over the pate and cover with 3–4 layers of foil. Bake at 180°C (350°F) for 1½ hours. Allow the pate to chill for 2 hours before turning out onto a serving dish. This pate is delicious served with a sauce made from onions, garlic and tomatoes.
Serves 4

HOT CHEESE BALLS

60 g butter
½ teaspoon prepared English mustard
freshly ground black pepper
5 tablespoons flour
2 cups milk
180 g Gruyere cheese
cornflour
2 eggs, beaten
dry breadcrumbs, to coat
oil for deep-frying

Melt the butter in a saucepan with the mustard and pepper. Stir in the flour and gradually add the milk. Continue stirring until the sauce thickens and boils. Pour the sauce into a bowl, cover with plastic wrap and cool.

Sprinkle a baking tray with cornflour. Cut the cheese into 1.5 cm cubes. Dip the cheese into the sauce so that each piece is coated and place them on the tray. Chill the balls until they are set.

Roll the cheese balls in beaten egg, then coat with breadcrumbs. Chill for half an hour.

Heat the oil and deep-fry the balls until golden brown. Drain and serve immediately.
Makes 12 balls

Vegetable Pate and Hot Cheese Balls

Prawn Pate (left) and Eggplant Puree

EGGPLANT PUREE

2 eggplants
juice 1 lemon
1 tablespoon oil
2 cloves garlic, crushed
125 g cream cheese
2 tablespoons yoghurt
black olives for decoration
paprika, to garnish

Place eggplants on a baking sheet and
cook for 1 hour in the oven at 180°C
(350°F). Cut in half, scoop out the pulp
and puree it in a blender or food
processor.

Add the lemon juice, oil, garlic,
cream cheese and yoghurt. Blend until
smooth. Place in a bowl and chill for
several hours. Garnish with olives and
paprika. Eggplant puree can be served
in the scooped out eggplant cases.
Serves 6–8

MELON AMBROSIA

1 rockmelon (cantaloupe)
1 honeydew melon

Dressing
2 teaspoons French mustard
1 teaspoon lemon juice
¼ teaspoon vanilla essence
6 tablespoons honey
150 mL mayonnaise
150 mL cream

Cut melons in half and scoop out seeds.
Use a melon baller to make as many
melon balls as you can. Mix them
together in a large bowl.

To make the dressing, blend mustard
with lemon juice and vanilla, stir in
honey, mayonnaise and cream. Serve
drizzled over the melon balls.
Serves 6–8

PRAWN PATE

500 g prawns, cooked and peeled
3 tablespoons lemon juice
½ cup olive oil
freshly ground black pepper
pinch paprika
dill, to garnish

Place the prawns in a blender or food
processor with the lemon juice and
puree. Slowly add the oil until well
blended. Add the seasonings. Chill
until needed. Garnish with dill and
serve with dry toast fingers.
Serves 6

TOMATO GRANITA

8 tomatoes, peeled and finely chopped
2 shallots, finely chopped
1 stick celery, finely chopped
1 clove garlic, crushed
1 cucumber
1 teaspoon chopped fresh mint
mint leaves for decoration

Strain the tomatoes to remove excess liquid and seeds. Mix the shallots, celery and garlic with the tomatoes and pour into ice cream trays. Freeze until solid.

Ten minutes before serving, remove from the freezer to soften a little. Peel the cucumber and chop into very fine dice. Break up the tomato ice with a fork and stir in the cucumber and mint. Serve in individual glass dishes. Garnish with mint leaves.
Serves 4

SPANAKOPITA

1 kg fresh spinach
7 eggs
250 g feta cheese, crumbled
125 g Cheddar cheese, grated
oil
1 onion, chopped
freshly ground black pepper
pinch dried oregano
8 sheets filo pastry
100 g butter

Wash the spinach well, chop it coarsely and put it into a large pan. Cover the pan and cook the spinach over low heat for 7–8 minutes or until it is wilted. Drain well in a colander, pressing out the moisture with a wooden spoon. Beat the eggs until fluffy and add the feta and Cheddar.

Heat a little oil in a pan and saute the onion until it is golden. Add the spin-ach, egg-cheese mixture, pepper and a little oregano.

Melt the butter and brush a baking dish with it. Lay a sheet of filo pastry on top and brush it with butter. Top with another 4 sheets, brushing each with melted butter and turning each sheet slightly so that the corners fan out, rather than stacking them on top of each other. Reserve 3 sheets.

Pour in the spinach mixture and fold the pastry ends over it. Butter the reserved sheets of filo and place them on the top to cover the dish. Slash the pastry in a few places with a sharp knife to allow the steam to escape. Brush the top with more melted butter and bake at 190°C (375°F) for 45 minutes.
Serves 8

ASPARAGUS WITH HERBS AND PARMESAN

Try to buy thick asparagus for this dish. However, if thin asparagus is all that's available, each diner will need 6 spears instead of 4, the stalks will not need peeling and the cooking time should be reduced to 7–9 minutes.

16 thick asparagus spears
80 g butter
1 clove garlic, finely chopped
1 tablespoon finely chopped fresh parsley
1 tablespoon finely chopped chives
1 tablespoon lemon juice
grated Parmesan cheese

Using a vegetable peeler, peel the lower part of the stalks, cut off the ends and wash the asparagus well in cold running water. Tie them into 2 bundles with string and place them in an asparagus steamer or a large pan of boiling water. The stalks only should be in the water so that the tips steam. Cover the pan with foil or an upturned saucepan of the same diameter. Cook for 10-15 minutes, depending upon the thickness of the asparagus. Test after 10 minutes; the thickest part of the stalk should be just tender. Overcooking ruins asparagus.

Drain and keep warm in a folded napkin. Melt the butter in a small frying pan over medium heat. Add the garlic, cook gently and stir in the herbs and lemon juice.

Place asparagus on warmed plates and pour the sauce over. Serve Parmesan separately.
Serves 4

Tomato Granita

Asparagus With Herbs and Parmesan

SPANISH-STYLE SARDINES

500 g sardines
olive oil, for shallow-frying
4 tablespoons flour
1 egg, beaten
lemon rind for decoration
oregano, to garnish

Marinade
1 teaspoon dry mustard
½ teaspoon freshly ground black
   pepper
1 tablespoon chopped fresh parsley
½ teaspoon dried oregano
3 tablespoons olive oil
juice ½ lemon
1 tablespoon chopped anchovy fillets

Split the sardines on one side and pull
out the backbone with the tail section.
Remove heads, rinse and dry.

Mix all the ingredients together for
the marinade and steep the sardines in
it for at least 1 hour.

Heat the oil, remove the sardines from
the marinade, dust very lightly with
flour and dip into beaten egg. Fry
quickly and serve hot, garnished with
lemon rind and oregano.
Serves 4

BRAINS IN BLACK BUTTER

4 sets brains
4 tablespoons vinegar
1 large onion, spiked with 4 cloves
1 bay leaf
2 tablespoons flour
100 g butter
1 tablespoon capers

Soak the brains in salted water for 1
hour, then remove and discard skins.
Place the brains in a saucepan and
cover with fresh water. Add vinegar,
onion and bay leaf, bring to the boil and
simmer for 15 minutes. Set aside in the
water, until ready to cook.

Remove the brains from the liquid,
pat them dry with a cloth, dust lightly
with flour and gently pan-fry in lots of
foaming butter, turning only once.

When they are cooked, remove them
with a slotted spoon and place on
warmed plates. Allow the butter to cook
briskly until it is dark, but not black.
Add the capers with a little of their brine
to the pan and pour over the brains.
Serve immediately with toast triangles.
Serves 4

GRILLED MUSHROOM CAPS

500 g medium-sized mushrooms
2–4 cloves garlic, crushed
60 g butter
2 tablespoons grated Parmesan cheese
4 tablespoons breadcrumbs
4 rashers bacon, trimmed and diced

Wipe mushrooms and carefully remove
the stalks. Chop the stalks finely and
mix them with the crushed garlic.

Mash the butter with a fork and mix in
the cheese, breadcrumbs and mushroom stalks. Fry or grill the bacon until
crisp, drain on kitchen paper and add to
the cheese mixture.

Fill the mushroom caps with the mixture and place under a hot grill to brown
quickly.
Serves 4–6

*Grilled Mushroom Caps and Spanish-
style Sardines*

RICE CROQUETTES WITH TOMATO SAUCE

2 cups cooked brown rice
½ cup grated Swiss cheese
1 tablespoon chopped chives
1 tablespoon grated carrot
1 tablespoon self-raising flour
¼ teaspoon chilli powder
freshly ground black pepper
2 eggs
oil for deep-frying

Tomato Sauce
¼ cup mayonnaise
¼ cup yoghurt
¼ cup sour cream
1 tablespoon tomato puree
¼ teaspoon cayenne pepper
chilli, shredded, to garnish

Combine rice, cheese, chives and carrot in a bowl. Mix in the flour, chilli powder and pepper. Separate the eggs and beat the yolks into the rice mixture. Beat the whites until stiff and fold into the rice mixture. Heat the oil for deep-frying and drop teaspoons of the mixture into it. Deep-fry until golden brown and serve warm with tomato sauce.

To make the tomato sauce, whisk all ingredients together until smooth. Chill before serving. Garnish with shredded chilli.
Serves 4

HERBED GREEN BEANS

125 g butter
½ teaspoon chopped fresh marjoram
½ teaspoon chopped fresh basil
1 teaspoon chopped fresh parsley
1 teaspoon chopped chives
500 g green beans
1 small onion, chopped
1 clove garlic, chopped
freshly ground black pepper
¼ cup sunflower seeds, to serve
fresh chives, to garnish

Combine butter with marjoram, basil, parsley and chives and set aside. Place the beans in a saucepan with the onion and garlic and cover with boiling water. Cook until tender and drain. Add herb butter to the pan and swirl the beans around briefly until well coated. Season to taste and add sunflower seeds just before serving. Tie beans into bundles with chives before serving.
Serves 6

Herbed Green Beans (above) and Rice Croquettes with Tomato Sauce

PIQUANT APRICOTS

250 g fresh apricots
125 g cream cheese
2 tablespoons mayonnaise
4 tablespoons chopped chives
1 tablespoon chopped fresh parsley
cayenne pepper
¼ red capsicum
fresh lettuce leaves

Cut the apricots in half and remove their stones. Beat the cheese with the mayonnaise and stir in the chives, parsley and pepper.

Spoon the mixture into the apricot halves. Cut the capsicum into thin strips and use it to garnish the apricots. Serve on a bed of shredded lettuce or in lettuce cups.
Serves 4

POTATOES CZARINA

6 large potatoes, baked in their skins
40 g butter
freshly ground black pepper
125 mL sour cream
small jar caviar or lumpfish roe
1 onion, finely chopped

Cut the tops off the baked potatoes and carefully scoop out the pulp into a warmed bowl. Mash, season and add butter and sour cream.

Carefully fold in caviar and onion and return to the potato cases. Heat through in the oven at 180°C (350°F).
Serves 6

HERBED JELLIED MEAT LOAF

1 cup mixed fresh herbs (parsley,
    tarragon and chives)
750 g cooked meat (chicken, turkey,
    ham, tongue or beef)
4–5 teaspoons green peppercorns,
    rinsed in cold water
500 mL chicken stock
5 teaspoons gelatine
½ cup white wine
juice 1 lemon
shredded lettuce, to serve

Finely chop the herbs and the meat and
mix them with the green peppercorns.
Put the stock into a saucepan and simmer. Dissolve the gelatine in the wine
and add to the stock with the lemon
juice. Pour it over the meat mixture.

Lightly oil a loaf tin and spoon the
mixture into it. Tap the tin on a bench to
eliminate air bubbles. Allow to cool,
then chill until set.

To unmould, run a warm knife around
the edges of the tin, cover with a serving
dish and turn upside down. Surround
with shredded lettuce and serve in
slices.
Serves 6–8

BROAD BEAN PATE

1 kg broad beans, shelled
125 g cream cheese
2 tablespoons chopped fresh parsley
juice 1 lemon
freshly ground black pepper

Cook the shelled beans in boiling water
until soft. Drain and pound to a paste
with a wooden spoon or in a food
processor. Beat in the cheese, parsley,
lemon juice and pepper. Press into an
earthenware bowl. Chill and serve with
hot toast.
Serves 6–8

TOMATOES ROQUEFORT

4 tomatoes, thinly sliced
1 thinly sliced onion, pushed into rings
1 tablespoon chopped fresh parsley
½ cup Roquefort cheese
2 tablespoons olive oil
2 tablespoons lemon juice
1 teaspoon sugar
freshly ground black pepper
pinch paprika

Place the tomatoes on a serving dish and
cover with a layer of onion rings. Blend
all the remaining ingredients until
creamy and pour over the tomato/onion
base. Chill before serving.
Serves 4

STUFFED TURNIPS

4 small turnips
40 g butter
sprig fresh rosemary
1 cup mashed potato
2 tablespoons grated onion
freshly ground black pepper
2 teaspoons chopped fresh parsley
juice 1 lemon

Wash the turnips, peel them, but do not
cut off the base. Cook the turnips in
boiling water until tender but still firm.
Cut a lid off each one and scoop out the
centre, leaving the outer part as a cup.
Reserve the pulp.

Melt the butter in a frying pan and
crumble the rosemary into it. Place the
turnip cups in the pan and cook for 1
minute.

Mash the turnip pulp with the potato
and add the grated onion and pepper.
Spoon the filling back into the turnip
cases, place in a baking dish and
sprinkle with parsley and lemon juice.
Bake at 200°C (400°F) for 10 minutes.
Serves 4

PRAWN RASCALS

1 cup chopped cooked prawns
1 sour apple, peeled and diced
½ cup chopped celery
¼ cup sliced radishes
1 tablespoon dried onion flakes
½ cup mayonnaise
4 tablespoons cream
1 tablespoon horseradish cream
2 tablespoons chopped walnuts
2–3 tomatoes, sliced thickly
freshly ground black pepper
1 tablespoon finely chopped fresh dill

Combine the prawns with the apple and
fresh vegetables in a bowl. In a separate
bowl mix together the onion flakes, mayonnaise, cream, horseradish and
walnuts. Add this to the prawn mixture
and season to taste.

To serve, place a spoonful of the
prawn mixture on top of each tomato
slice and sprinkle with dill.
Serves 4–6

POTATO SOUFFLE

500 g potatoes, boiled
20 g butter
4 tablespoons cream
3 egg yolks, whisked
freshly ground black pepper
4 tablespoons grated Cheddar cheese
4 egg whites, stiffly beaten

Mash potatoes well with butter and
cream. Add the whisked egg yolks,
season to taste and stir in most of the
cheese, retaining a little for the topping.

Fold in stiffly beaten egg whites. Pour
into a buttered souffle dish and sprinkle
with the remaining cheese. Bake at
190°C (375°F) for 25 minutes and serve
immediately from the souffle dish.
Serves 4–6

STUFFED ARTICHOKES

4 artichokes
4 lemon slices
2 tablespoons white wine vinegar
6 hard-boiled eggs, chopped
3 shallots, chopped
5 tomatoes, peeled, seeded and
 chopped

Dressing
150 mL natural yoghurt
1 teaspoon honey
1 teaspoon Dijon mustard
1 tablespoon oil
juice 1 lemon
1 tablespoon chopped fresh parsley

Remove the stems from the artichokes and cut the base flush so that it will sit up straight on a plate. Using a very sharp knife, cut the top off the artichoke, about ¼ of the way down.

Stand each artichoke on a slice of lemon in a saucepan and cook in boiling salted water for 15–20 minutes. Drain.

To make the dressing, mix all the ingredients together in a screw-top jar. Mix with the eggs, shallots and tomatoes.

Gently open the artichoke leaves to reveal the hairy choke in the centre. Scoop this out with a teaspoon and discard. Spoon the filling into the artichoke hearts and serve at room temperature or slightly chilled.

To eat, break off the leaves, one by one, starting with the large outside leaves. Dip the base of the leaf into the filling and pull the leaf between your teeth, eating only the fleshy base and discarding the stringy leaf tops.
Serves 4

Stuffed Artichokes

SALADS

Most of the salads in this chapter are main courses in themselves. Made in smaller quantities, they can be served as a first course, American style.

The flavour of many salads is improved if they are served warm or at room temperature instead of cold. Chicken salad, for example, is delicious if served at room temperature; it suffers badly once it has been chilled. The same applies to seafood salads. However, if a salad is not to be chilled, it must be served soon after it is made, especially in summer.

There are no recipes here for simple green salads, although these are mentioned often in the menus at the back of the book. To make a green salad, wash lettuce leaves, either one type or several types such as cos, mignonette and butter, drain them well in a colander, salad basket or, best of all, salad twirler, tear the leaves and dress with a mixture of oil and vinegar or lemon juice. The usual proportions are 5 parts oil to 1 part vinegar, but you can change that to suit your own taste. Add mustard if you like, with salt and pepper. A more complicated green salad includes chicory, endive, spinach, watercress or any other green leaves. The torn leaves of fresh herbs, especially parsley, basil and salad burnet make a delicious addition.

POPPY SEED SALAD

1 lettuce
4 leaves spinach
1 cucumber, peeled and diced
½ green capsicum, thinly sliced
½ cup chopped shallots

Dressing
¼ cup sugar
2 teaspoons dry mustard
3 tablespoons lemon juice
4 tablespoons poppy seeds
1 cup white wine vinegar
¾ cup olive oil

Wash lettuce and spinach thoroughly and tear into bite-sized pieces. Combine with cucumber, capsicum and shallots in a salad bowl and refrigerate while preparing the dressing.

Mix together sugar, mustard, lemon juice, poppy seeds and vinegar. Gradually beat in the oil until the dressing is thick.

Use as much dressing as required for the salad and store the rest in a screw top jar.
Serves 4

BEAN SALAD

½ cup cooked kidney beans
½ cup cooked soybeans
½ cup cooked lima beans
1 cup cooked green beans
1 tablespoon chopped parsley
1 cup shredded cabbage
½ cup chopped onion
2 tablespoons olive oil
4 tablespoons white wine vinegar
freshly ground black pepper

Mix together the beans, parsley, cabbage and onion in a salad bowl. Beat the oil into the vinegar and add pepper. Pour over salad and chill well before serving.
Serves 4

TROPICAL RICE SALAD

1 lettuce
2 cups cooked brown rice
1 cup chopped pineapple
¼ cup chopped celery
¼ cup chopped shallots
¼ cup chopped red capsicum
¼ cup corn kernels
¼ cup chopped walnuts
1 red apple
2 tablespoons lemon juice
1 tomato
1 tablespoon chopped fresh parsley

Wash the lettuce and line a salad bowl with the best leaves. Shred the remaining lettuce. Mix together the rice, pineapple, celery, shallots, capsicum, corn, walnuts and shredded lettuce. Add to the lettuce-lined salad bowl and chill.

Core the apple, chop it into cubes and mix with lemon juice to prevent it from browning. Add it to the salad. Cut the tomato into wedges and place them around the edge of the bowl. Sprinkle with parsley and serve.
Serves 4

POTATO NUT SALAD

250 g new potatoes
1 tablespoon olive oil
2 sticks celery, chopped
1 green apple
1 tablespoon lemon juice
¼ cup pine nuts
¼ cup chopped shallots
¼ cup chopped red capsicum
½ cup yoghurt
1 tablespoon tomato puree
freshly ground black pepper
¼ teaspoon dry mustard
1 tablespoon pine nuts, toasted in the oven

Boil the potatoes in their jackets until they are tender. Cool, peel and chop into small cubes. Pour the oil over them and mix gently. Add the celery to the potatoes. Core the unpeeled apple and chop it into small cubes. Toss in lemon juice to prevent browning, then add to potatoes.

Place the potato mixture into a salad bowl and stir in the pine nuts, shallots and capsicum. Cover and chill while you make the dressing.

Beat together the yoghurt, tomato puree, pepper and mustard. Pour over the salad, mix well and serve garnished with toasted pine nuts.
Serves 4

Orange and Avocado Salad

RUSSIAN RED CABBAGE SALAD

6 cups shredded red cabbage
1 cinnamon stick
1 cup apple cider vinegar
1 green apple
2 tablespoons lemon juice
1 cup sliced mushrooms
½ cup grated onion
3 tablespoons yoghurt
freshly ground black pepper
¼ teaspoon prepared mustard

Put the cabbage in a bowl with the cinnamon stick. Heat the vinegar, pour it over the cabbage, cover the bowl and allow to stand until cold. Drain off the liquid and remove the cinnamon stick.

Peel, core and cut the apples into cubes, then sprinkle with 1 tablespoon of lemon juice to prevent browning. Combine the cabbage, apple, mushrooms and onion in a salad bowl.

Mix the remaining lemon juice, yoghurt, pepper and mustard together and pour over the salad just before serving.
Serves 4

Springtime Salad

SPRINGTIME SALAD

3 cups cauliflower florets
1 avocado
juice 1 lemon
1 cup asparagus pieces
1 lettuce
¼ cup chopped shallots
1 tablespoon olive oil
4 tablespoons tarragon vinegar
1 teaspoon chopped fresh parsley
freshly ground black pepper
¼ teaspoon prepared mustard
toasted sesame seeds, to garnish

Steam cauliflower until tender but still crisp. Refresh under cold water and pat dry. Halve the avocado, peel and remove seed. Cut it into cubes and sprinkle with lemon juice to prevent browning.

Cover asparagus pieces with boiling water, cook for 5 minutes, refresh under cold water and pat dry. Wash and shred the lettuce.

Combine cauliflower, avocado, asparagus and shallots and chill.

Mix together the oil, vinegar, parsley, pepper and mustard. Pour it over the salad, toss and serve on a bed of lettuce leaves garnished with toasted sesame seeds.
Serves 4

ORANGE AND AVOCADO SALAD

4 oranges, chilled
1 large avocado
juice 1–2 limes
2 teaspoons French mustard
watercress sprigs, to garnish

Peel the oranges and carefully remove all the white pith. With a very sharp knife, segment each orange and remove pips, being careful to retain any juices that squeeze out. Arrange the orange segments on 4 plates.

Segment the avocado. Whisk the lime juice, adding mustard and a little orange juice. Arrange the avocado on each plate with the orange slices. Drizzle the lime dressing over the avocado and orange and serve topped with sprigs of watercress.
Serves 4

ORANGE AND SPINACH SALAD

½ bunch spinach, torn
4 shallots, chopped
¼ cup toasted flaked almonds
2 oranges, peeled and segmented
2 tablespoons olive oil
1 tablespoon vinegar
1 tablespoon lemon juice
freshly ground black pepper
pinch dry mustard

Wash the spinach and remove stalks. Shred it and drain in a colander.

Mix together the spinach, shallots and almonds and place on a serving dish. Arrange the sliced oranges over the spinach.

Combine the oil, vinegar, lemon juice, pepper and mustard and pour it over the salad. Chill for 1 hour before serving.
Serves 4

WALDORF SALAD WITH PEAS

4 green apples
juice 2 lemons
½ lettuce, shredded
1 cup cooked peas
½ cup chopped celery
½ cup chopped walnuts
2 tablespoons olive oil
3 tablespoons white wine vinegar
¼ teaspoon prepared mustard
freshly ground black pepper

Peel, core and dice the apples and pour lemon juice over them to prevent them from browning.

Wash and shred the lettuce and combine with the apples, peas, celery and walnuts in a salad bowl.

Mix together the oil, vinegar, mustard and pepper and pour over the salad. Toss and serve.
Serves 4

CURRIED BROWN RICE SALAD

3 cups cooked brown rice
½ cup diced red capsicum
½ cup canned corn kernels, drained
¼ cup chopped shallots
freshly ground black pepper
¼ cup chopped celery
2 tablespoons salad oil
1 tablespoon tarragon vinegar
1 teaspoon chopped fresh parsley
2 teaspoons curry powder

Mix together the rice, capsicum, corn, shallots, pepper and celery in a salad bowl. Combine the oil, vinegar, parsley and curry powder and pour over the salad. Toss well and serve.
Serves 4-6

FARMHOUSE SALAD

350 g cream cheese
1 cup grated Cheddar cheese
¼ cup cream
¼ cup chopped red capsicum
¼ cup chopped shallots
¼ cup pine nuts
3 teaspoons lemon juice
¼ teaspoon paprika
1 lettuce
3 tomatoes
1 tablespoon chopped chives

Beat the cream cheese until smooth, add Cheddar and cream and mix until well blended. Stir in the capsicum, shallots, pine nuts, lemon juice and paprika. Spread the mixture in a freezer tray and chill until firm.

Wash and shred the lettuce and cut the tomatoes into wedges. Place the lettuce on a serving dish and arrange the tomato wedges on top.

Remove the cheese from the freezer, cut into cubes and place them on the salad. Sprinkle with chives and serve.
Serves 4

ZUCCHINI AND CHEESE SALAD

250 g zucchini
4 celery stalks, cut in strips
1 cup diced Gruyere cheese
12 small radishes, cut in half
¼ cup walnuts, roughly chopped
1 teaspoon French mustard
4 tablespoons mayonnaise
juice ½ lemon
endives, to garnish

Cut zucchini diagonally into 1 cm slices. Blanch in boiling, salted water for 1 minute. Drain and plunge into iced water. Pat dry on kitchen paper.

Mix zucchini with celery, cheese, radishes and walnuts in a bowl. Whisk the mustard into the mayonnaise and add lemon juice. Drizzle the mayonnaise mixture onto the salad and serve garnished with endives.
Serves 4-6

MACARONI AND ZUCCHINI SALAD

250 g zucchini
salt
1 cup sliced mushrooms
1 cup cooked wholemeal macaroni
¾ cup cream
¼ cup crunchy peanut butter
½ cup mayonnaise
1 tablespoon honey
1 tablespoon white wine vinegar
1 tablespoon lemon juice
½ cup roasted peanuts

Wash and slice the zucchini. Place it on kitchen paper, sprinkle with salt and allow to stand for 30 minutes. Rinse under cold water and pat dry. Combine the zucchini, mushrooms and macaroni in a salad bowl and chill while you prepare the dressing.

Place all the remaining ingredients except the peanuts in a blender and whip until smooth but not too thick. Coat the salad lightly with the dressing. Chill well and serve garnished with roasted peanuts. Any leftover dressing will keep for 2 days in the refrigerator.
Serves 4-6

Orange and Spinach Salad (above) and Zucchini and Cheese Salad

Fruit and Nut Salad

FRUIT AND NUT SALAD

2 grapefruit, segmented
2 oranges, segmented
1 cup chopped fresh pineapple
1 large green apple, chopped
1 tablespoon lemon juice
½ cup stuffed olives
½ lettuce
¼ cup toasted almonds
¼ cup chopped walnuts
1 tablespoon olive oil
2 tablespoons white wine vinegar
freshly ground black pepper
1 tablespoon chopped chives

Mix together the grapefruit, oranges and pineapple in a bowl and chill. Toss the apples in lemon juice to prevent browning and add to other fruit with the olives.

Wash the lettuce, place the leaves on a serving dish and spoon the fruit mixture on top. Sprinkle with nuts.

Combine the oil, vinegar, pepper and chives and pour over the salad just before serving.
Serves 4

WARM BEETROOT SALAD

1 kg beetroot
5 tablespoons good salad oil
1 tablespoon white wine vinegar
freshly ground black pepper
1 tablespoon fennel, grated
1 large onion, sliced
40 g butter
chives, to garnish

Top and tail the beetroot, wrap each one in foil and bake at 180°C (350°F) for an hour or until they are tender when tested with a toothpick. Cool until you can handle them and peel off their skin.

Cut beetroot into strips. Mix together the oil, vinegar and pepper and pour over the beetroot. You may not need all of it. Sprinkle with fennel.

Fry the onion in the butter until it is golden. Pour over the beetroot and mix gently. Garnish with chives.
Serves 6–8

SICILIAN FENNEL SALAD

1 clove garlic, crushed
1 cucumber, seeds removed and thinly sliced
1 onion, thinly sliced
1 peeled orange, segmented
4 tomatoes, sliced
1 bulb fennel, sliced
1 tablespoon oil
2 tablespoons lemon juice
freshly ground black pepper
½ teaspoon chopped basil
fresh basil, to garnish

Sprinkle the garlic over a serving dish. Layer the prepared salad vegetables on the platter and chill. Mix together the oil, lemon juice, pepper and basil, pour over the salad and serve. Garnish with basil.
Serves 4

*Warm Beetroot Salad (above) and
Sicilian Fennel Salad without tomato
and onion*

MEATLESS MAIN COURSES

This chapter is the heart of the book. It will show those who have always eaten meat and two vegetables for dinner that there are a number of interesting alternatives, and it will give confirmed vegetarians a few new ideas.

The key to good nutrition is variety. This book is not a vegetarian cookbook, because it recognises that most people still include meat in their diet. However, by cooking meatless main courses sometimes, you'll not only get out of your lamb chops rut, you'll naturally become healthier from the grains, pulses and vegetables that you may not have tried before.

TOFU SPINACH SOUFFLE

500 g spinach
1 tablespoon oil or ghee
1 teaspoon dried thyme
1 teaspoon dried oregano
150 g tofu
1 teaspoon kelp powder
6 tablespoons water
½ teaspoon freshly ground black pepper
4 egg whites

Remove the stalks from the spinach, wash it well and chop it very finely with a sharp knife or in a food processor.

Heat the oil in a pan and cook the spinach for 5 minutes with the thyme and oregano. Drain off excess liquid by pressing between two plates.

Liquidise tofu with kelp and water in a food processor or blender and add the pepper. Mix with the spinach and leave to cool.

Whisk the egg whites until they form stiff peaks and gently fold them through the spinach mixture. Lightly oil a souffle dish and fill with the spinach mixture. Bake at 190°C (375°F) for 30–35 minutes until it is well risen and firm to the touch. Serve immediately.
Serves 4

CRUNCHY NUT TERRINE

1 tablespoon oil
1½ cups chopped celery
1½ cups chopped onion
½ cup almond meal
1 cup chopped walnuts
1 cup toasted, chopped cashew nuts
¼ cup rolled oats
1 tablespoon sesame seeds
250 g cottage cheese
3 eggs
¼ teaspoon freshly ground black pepper
1 teaspoon chopped fresh parsley
¼ teaspoon dried marjoram

Heat the oil and cook the celery and onion until golden. Drain and place in a bowl with all the remaining ingredients. Mix thoroughly.

Grease two 10 x 23 cm loaf tins, and line with greaseproof paper. Spoon half the mixture into each. Bake at 180°C (350°F) for 45 minutes and test for firmness by pressing lightly with your finger. If the terrine is not firm, bake for a further 5–8 minutes.

Leave to cool slightly in the pan, then turn out onto a plate and remove the paper. Serve hot or cold with a salad.
Serves 8–10

SPICY BEAN SPROUTS

500 g fresh bean sprouts
20 g butter
1 teaspoon minced ginger root
1 teaspoon crushed garlic
2 onions, finely chopped
½ teaspoon turmeric
1 teaspoon cumin
¼ teaspoon paprika
1 teaspoon minced red chilli

Wash the bean sprouts and drain well. Heat the butter in a frying pan and cook the ginger and garlic for 1 minute. Add the onions and cook for 3 minutes. Add the turmeric, cumin, paprika and chilli and cook for 3 minutes. Stir in the sprouts, mix well and cook for 3 minutes.
Serves 4

BRAISED CHINESE VEGETABLES

¼ cup oil
1 teaspoon grated ginger root
1 clove garlic, crushed
1 large onion, cut into eighths
1 carrot, sliced
1 stick celery, sliced
1 red capsicum, chopped
½ green capsicum, chopped
2 small zucchini, sliced
200 g snow peas, strung
1 cup water chestnuts, halved
1 cup bamboo shoots, sliced
1 cup broccoli florets
½ cup chicken stock
1 tablespoon soy sauce
½ teaspoon sesame oil
½ teaspoon chilli sauce
3 tablespoons bean sprouts
shallot curls, to garnish

Heat the oil in a large frying pan or wok, add the ginger and garlic and cook until golden. Add the onion pieces, carrot and celery and stir over high heat. Add the capsicums, zucchini, snow peas, water chestnuts, bamboo shoots and broccoli and toss gently until heated through.

Lower the heat, pour in the stock, soy sauce, sesame oil and chilli sauce and stir until combined. Cover and heat gently for 2 minutes or until the vegetables are tender but still crisp. Add bean sprouts and serve garnished with shallot curls.
Serves 4

HOT RICE SALAD

1 cup cooked brown rice
40 g butter
1 onion, chopped
60 g snow peas
¼ cup chopped red capsicum
1 zucchini, sliced
2 spinach leaves, finely chopped
red capsicum, cut in strips, to garnish

Dressing
2 hard-boiled eggs, chopped
freshly ground black pepper
¼ teaspoon paprika
½ cup sour cream

Keep the cooked rice hot in a colander over hot water. Melt the butter in a frying pan and add the onion, snow peas, capsicum and zucchini. Cook for 5 minutes and mix with the hot rice. Add the spinach to the rice.

To make the dressing, place the chopped eggs in a saucepan with the pepper, paprika and sour cream. Heat but do not boil. Place the salad in a serving bowl and pour over the sour cream dressing. Garnish with strips of red capsicum.
Serves 4

BEAN AND VEGETABLE TACOS

1 tablespoon oil
6 shallots, finely chopped
1 clove garlic, crushed
1 carrot, finely chopped
1 stick celery, finely chopped
300 g canned red kidney beans
2 cups fresh or canned tomato sauce
chilli sauce, to taste
8 taco shells
Cheddar cheese, grated
2 tomatoes, diced
lettuce leaves, finely shredded

Heat the oil in a frying pan and add the shallots, garlic, carrot and celery. Cook over low heat, stirring, for 5 minutes, then add the kidney beans and squash them with the back of a wooden spoon. Add the tomato sauce and chilli sauce, reduce the heat and simmer for 10 minutes. Add a little water if the mixture starts to thicken too much.

Meanwhile, put the taco shells upside down on the rungs of the oven rack and heat at 180°C (350°F) for 8–10 minutes. Spoon some of the bean mixture into each taco shell, top with grated cheese, then diced tomato and shredded lettuce.
Serves 4

ONION AND NUT PIE

150 g carrots, diced finely
1 kg onions, thinly sliced
250 g mushrooms, sliced
6 green cabbage leaves
2 eggs
1 tablespoon milk powder
½ cup water
¼ teaspoon dried thyme
2 tablespoons pine nuts
2 tablespoons hazelnuts
2 tablespoons cashews
40 g margarine
2 cups soft brown breadcrumbs
1 teaspoon yeast extract
1 teaspoon chopped chives
1 teaspoon chopped fresh parsley

Place the carrots in a large saucepan with a little water and cook for 5 minutes. Drain off the water and add the onions to the pan. Cover and cook over gentle heat for 5 minutes, stirring often to prevent them from sticking or browning. Add the mushrooms and cook for a further minute. Do not allow them to brown.

Remove the hard stems from the cabbage leaves and plunge them into boiling water for 4 minutes. Remove, rinse under cold water and pat dry. Line a greased 20 cm spring-form tin with cabbage leaves, allowing the leaves to hang over the edge of the tin.

Mix together the eggs, milk powder, water and thyme and stir into the onion mixture. Spoon the filling evenly into the prepared cake tin and trim the cabbage leaves to be level with the top of the filling.

Grind all the nuts in a blender and mix with the remaining ingredients. Sprinkle this topping over the onion filling.

Place the cake tin in a baking dish half-filled with cold water and bake at 200°C (400°F) for 1 hour. Remove the tin from the water and allow to stand for 5 minutes before opening the sides of the tin. Serve warm, in slices.
Serves 6

Hot Rice Salad

CASHEW NUT ROAST

oil
1–2 tablespoons dried breadcrumbs
75 g butter
1 onion, finely chopped
100 g mushrooms, sliced
¼ teaspoon dried marjoram
125 g rolled oats
300 mL milk
1 egg, beaten
freshly ground black pepper
250 g raw unsalted cashew nuts, very
    finely chopped
fresh marjoram, to garnish

Lightly oil a 1 kg loaf tin and coat with breadcrumbs. Melt the butter and saute the onion and mushrooms for 2 minutes. Add the marjoram and rolled oats and gradually add the milk, stirring continuously. Cool slightly, then stir in the egg and nuts. Season to taste. The mixture should be a soft dropping consistency.

Pour it into the tin and smooth over the top with a spatula. Bake at 180°C (350°F) for 1¼ hours. Garnish with marjoram.
Serves 6

ORIENTAL BROWN RICE

250 g long-grain brown rice
3 tablespoons oil
16 shallots, chopped
1 clove garlic, crushed
2 tablespoons grated ginger
4 sticks celery, diced
150 g can water chestnuts, sliced
500 g bean sprouts
3 tablespoons chopped parsley
1 teaspoon dried oregano
½ teaspoon dried basil
½ cup sunflower seeds
½ cup honey
⅓ cup soy sauce
1 tablespoon lemon juice
310 g can mandarines, drained

Cook the rice until tender in boiling water and drain well. Heat the oil in a wok or large frying pan and add the shallots, garlic and ginger. Saute for 1 minute. Add the celery, water chestnuts, bean sprouts and parsley and stir-fry for 1 minute. Add the herbs and sunflower seeds.

Mix together the honey, soy sauce and lemon juice and stir into the vegetables. Add the rice and mandarines and heat through gently.
Serves 6

Spanish Omelette (above) and Cashew Nut Roast

MUGHAL VEGETABLES

3 tablespoons oil
2 onions, sliced
seeds from 6 cardamon pods
5 cm stick cinnamon, broken
2 tablespoons poppy seeds
¾ teaspoon chilli powder
¼ teaspoon ground cloves
250 g cauliflower florets
250 g zucchini, sliced
175 g carrots, sliced
175 g green beans, sliced
100 g mushrooms, sliced
⅓ cup desiccated coconut
¼ cup slivered almonds
¼ cup pistachio nuts (optional)
2 cups beef stock
150 mL sour cream
2 teaspoons lemon juice

Heat the oil in a large saucepan and saute the onions until they are soft but not brown. Add spices, vegetables, nuts and stock and season to taste. Bring to the boil, cover and simmer for 15 minutes or until the vegetables are tender.

Using a slotted spoon, transfer the vegetables to a serving dish and keep them warm. Add sour cream and lemon juice to the liquid, reheat and spoon over the vegetables.
Serves 4

BROAD BEAN CASSEROLE

3 cups shelled broad beans
20 g butter
1 bay leaf
1 cup tomato relish (see below)
pinch dried basil

Cook the broad beans in a small amount of boiling water until they are just tender. Drain and place in a casserole dish with all the other ingredients. Cover and bake at 180°C (350°F) for 15 minutes. Remove cover and continue cooking for another 15 minutes.
Serves 4

TOMATO RELISH

4 under-ripe tomatoes, peeled and
    chopped
1 onion, chopped
1 stick celery, chopped
¼ cup horseradish cream
1 teaspoon prepared French mustard
1 tablespoon brown sugar
1 cup malt vinegar

To make the tomato relish, place all the ingredients in a saucepan, cover and simmer for 45 minutes. Spoon the mixture into sterilised warm jars, seal and store in the refrigerator.

SPANISH OMELETTE

3 tablespoons olive oil
1 large peeled potato, diced small
1 large Spanish onion, finely chopped
5 eggs
freshly ground black pepper

Heat the oil in a large frying pan. Saute the potato and onion, stirring occasionally, until both are cooked but not brown. Whisk the eggs with pepper and pour it into the pan, spreading evenly. Cover the pan, lower the heat and allow the omelette to cook for about 10 minutes.

Place a plate of a similar size to your frying pan over the top of it and invert the omelette. Return it immediately to the pan and allow the other side to brown. It will be thick and golden in colour when it is ready.
Serves 4

CHEESY CARROT RING

40 g butter
1 kg young carrots, finely chopped
freshly ground black pepper
1 cup chicken or vegetable stock
125 g button mushrooms, chopped
1 teaspoon olive oil
2 eggs, beaten
¼ cup grated Edam cheese
1 teaspoon chopped fresh dill

Heat the butter in a pan, add the carrots and brown lightly. Add pepper and stock, cover the pan and simmer for 30 minutes. Fry the mushrooms in olive oil for 3 minutes, then drain.

Combine carrots and mushrooms in a bowl, with eggs, cheese and dill. Grease a ring tin and line with greaseproof paper. Spoon the mixture into the tin and press down firmly. Cover with foil and place in a baking dish with 3 cm water.

Bake at 200°C (400°F) for 20 minutes, reduce heat to 180°C (350°F) and bake for a further 20 minutes. Allow to stand for 10 minutes before turning out onto a serving dish.
Serves 6

EGGPLANT AND WALNUT PUFF

500 g eggplant
40 g butter
2 tablespoons flour
1 cup milk
4 eggs, separated
2 tablespoons chopped walnuts
pinch grated nutmeg
freshly ground black pepper

Bake the whole eggplant at 200°C (400°F) for 30 minutes or until pulp is soft. Meanwhile, melt the butter in a pan, stir in the flour and cook for 1 minute. Gradually add the milk, stirring continuously until thick and smooth. Remove the sauce from the heat and stir in lightly beaten egg yolks with walnuts, nutmeg and pepper.

Split the eggplant, scrape out the pulp, mash well and stir it into the sauce. Beat the egg whites until stiff and fold them into the sauce.

Pour the mixture into an oiled souffle dish and bake at 190°C (375°F) for 45 minutes. Serve immediately.
Serves 4

CABBAGE CAKE

4 large green cabbage leaves
3 cups chopped green vegetables
(spinach, sorrel, Chinese cabbage, leeks, onions, shallots)
1 egg
1 egg white
2 tablespoons plain yoghurt
2 tablespoons cottage cheese
1 tablespoon mixed fresh herbs (chives, parsley, tarragon)
freshly ground black pepper

Remove the thick stalks from the cabbage leaves and blanch for 2–3 minutes in boiling water. Drain. Blanch green vegetables for 2–3 minutes and drain. Blanch the onions and leeks for 2–3 minutes and drain.

Line a 15 cm cake tin with the cabbage leaves, with the tips in the centre and the base of the leaves hanging over the edge of the tin. They must be large enough to cover the contents of the tin once the filling has been added.

Mix the blanched vegetables together and spoon into the tin. Combine the remaining ingredients, beating well. Pour the filling over the vegetables and enclose with the cabbage leaves.

Cover with foil and place in a baking dish half-filled with water. Bake at 180°C (350°F) for 1 hour. Remove and allow to rest for 15 minutes before turning it out of the cake tin. Slice and serve with fresh tomato sauce.
Serves 4

ZYLDYK CASSEROLE

250 g spinach
2 carrots, sliced
1 large zucchini, sliced
1 large onion, sliced
175 g cauliflower florets
175 g cabbage, shredded
25 g butter
1 tablespoon flour
750 mL skim milk
175 g Edam cheese, finely grated
2 teaspoons curry powder
2 slices wholemeal bread, crumbed

Remove stalks from the spinach and cook in a little water for 10 minutes. Place the carrots, zucchini, onion, cauliflower and cabbage in a saucepan and barely cover with water. Bring to the boil, then drain, reserving 150 mL of the liquid.

Place the vegetables in an ovenproof dish and arrange the spinach on top. Melt the butter, stir in the flour and cook for 1 minute. Gradually stir in the reserved vegetable liquid and the milk. Bring to the boil and simmer for 2 minutes, stirring continuously.

Add 100 g cheese and all the curry powder and stir well. Spoon the sauce over the vegetables. Mix together the remaining cheese and the breadcrumbs and sprinkle over the dish. Bake at 190°C (375°F) for 30 minutes.
Serves 4

INSTANT BEAN MEDLEY

1 tablespoon oil
1 onion, chopped
1 red capsicum, chopped
445 g can soybeans
465 g can red kidney beans
310 g can lima beans
310 g can butter beans
285 g can champignon mushrooms
440 g can corn kernels
310 g can asparagus cuts
425 g can whole tomatoes
freshly ground black pepper
½ teaspoon chilli powder
1 tablespoon chopped chives
1 cup grated Cheddar cheese
½ cup soft breadcrumbs

Heat the oil and saute the onion and capsicum until the onion is soft but not brown. Drain all the cans of their liquid and mix together all the ingredients except the cheese and breadcrumbs. Spoon into a greased casserole.

Mix together the cheese and breadcrumbs and sprinkle on top. Bake at 190°C (375°F) for 20 minutes, then place the casserole under the griller to brown the top before serving.
Serves 4–6

STIR-FRY TOFU

2 cups boiling water
1 cup bean sprouts
150 g tofu
¼ cup vegetable oil
1 clove garlic, crushed
1 teaspoon grated fresh ginger root
4 shallots, cut in 2.5 cm (1 inch) lengths
6 small mushrooms, sliced
½ red capsicum, cut in thin strips
½ teaspoon soy sauce

Pour boiling water over the bean sprouts, leave to stand for 2 minutes, then drain. Rinse the tofu in hot water, drain on paper towels and cut into 2.5 cm (1 inch) cubes.

Heat the oil in a frying pan and add the garlic, ginger, shallots, mushrooms and capsicum. Cook for about 6 minutes, stirring from time to time. Add all the remaining ingredients, heat through and serve immediately.
Serves 2

OKRA CASSEROLE

1 eggplant
salt
2 carrots, sliced
2 potatoes, peeled and sliced
2 onions, sliced
¼ cup olive oil
4 zucchini, sliced
4 tomatoes, sliced
2 cups okra, canned or fresh
¼ cup chopped fresh parsley
2 teaspoons dried oregano
freshly ground black pepper
¼ teaspoon nutmeg

Slice the eggplant, sprinkle with salt and leave to stand in a colander for 30 minutes. Simmer the carrots and potatoes in water for 5 minutes. Drain and rinse under cold water. Rinse the eggplant and pat dry.

Heat the oil and saute the onions until soft but not brown. Remove with a slotted spoon and add the eggplant. Fry until golden on both sides. Top and tail the okra.

In a deep casserole dish, layer all the vegetables, sprinkling each layer with a little parsley, oregano, pepper and nutmeg. Cover the casserole and bake at 190°C (375°F) for 1 hour or until tender.
Serves 6

VEGETABLE STRUDEL

2 carrots, thinly sliced
250 g green beans
260 g broccoli florets
1 leek
30 g butter
4 medium-sized mushrooms, sliced
1 stick celery, finely chopped
125 g bean sprouts
5 sheets filo pastry
60 g butter, melted
125 g grated Cheddar cheese
125 g fresh breadcrumbs

freshly ground black pepper
1 tablespoon finely chopped fresh basil
fresh chervil, to garnish
carrot, cut in straws, to garnish

Blanch the carrots for 2 minutes in boiling water, drain and set aside. Top, tail and slice the beans and cook for 3 minutes in boiling water, drain and set aside. Boil broccoli florets for 3 minutes, drain and set aside.

Wash the leek well and slice the white part very finely. Melt the butter and cook the leek over low heat until it is soft. Add the mushrooms to the pan. Cook for 1 minute, then add the celery and cook for 1 minute. Add the bean sprouts and the reserved vegetables and toss well. Allow to cool.

Brush 5 sheets of filo pastry with melted butter and place them one on top of the other. Mix together the cheese and breadcrumbs and sprinkle half over the top layer of pastry. Add the vegetables in a layer and sprinkle with the remaining cheese and crumbs. Season with pepper and basil.

Roll up the pastry, seal and brush with melted butter. Bake at 190°C (375°F) for 35 minutes. Before serving, decorate with chervil and carrot straws.
Serves 6

Vegetable Strudel

SPINACH TARTS

Pastry

1¼ cups flour
¼ teaspoon salt
60 g butter, diced
40 g lard, diced
2 tablespoons iced water
fresh watercress, to garnish
cherry tomatoes, to garnish

Filling

40 g butter
3 tablespoons chopped shallots
1½ cups spinach, cooked and drained
   (or 1 packet frozen spinach)
dash nutmeg
freshly ground black pepper
250 g cream cheese
4 eggs
½ cup cream

To make the pastry, put the flour into a bowl with the salt. Using your fingertips, rub the butter and lard into the flour until the mixture resembles coarse breadcrumbs. Add water and knead lightly. Form the dough into a ball, dust with flour, wrap in grease-proof paper and chill for 1 hour.

Roll the dough out thinly and line 6 small flan dishes. Prick the base of the shells and chill for 1 hour while preparing the filling.

To make the filling, melt the butter in a pan over medium heat and add the shallots. When soft, add the spinach, nutmeg and pepper. Cook for 5 minutes.

Place in a bowl and beat in the cream cheese. Separate the eggs, add 4 yolks, one at a time to the spinach. Add the cream. In another bowl, beat the egg whites until stiff and fold them into the spinach mixture.

Cover the base of the flan with grease-proof paper and dried beans or rice and bake it blind at 200°C (400°F) for 15 minutes. Remove beans and paper and allow the pastry shells to cool.

Fill with the spinach mixture, dot with butter and bake at 180°C (350°F) for 15-20 minutes. Allow to cool before serving. Garnish with watercress and cherry tomatoes.
Serves 6

BOLIVIAN BEAN STEW

1 cup butter beans
1 cup chick peas
chicken stock
1 cup lentils
1 green capsicum, roughly chopped
1 red capsicum, roughly chopped
4 sticks celery, thickly sliced
2 carrots, chopped
250 g tomatoes, peeled
310 g can corn kernels, drained
2 tablespoons tomato paste
bouquet garni

Soak the beans and chick peas overnight in water to cover. Drain and measure liquid, adding chicken stock to make up to 600 mL.

Place all the ingredients in a saucepan and bring to the boil very slowly — it should take about 30 minutes — then simmer for 1-1½ hours or until the beans and chick peas are tender. Remove the bouquet garni and season to taste.
Serves 6

VEGETABLE CURRY

⅓ cup oil
2 teaspoons cumin
½ teaspoon turmeric
¼ teaspoon chilli powder
2 large onions, chopped
2 cloves garlic, crushed
small piece ginger root, grated
2 large tomatoes, peeled and chopped
4 potatoes, quartered
¼ head cauliflower, cut into florets
3-4 zucchini, sliced
½ eggplant, diced
1 cup frozen peas
½ cup water

Heat the oil and stir in the cumin, turmeric and chilli powder. Add the onions, garlic and ginger and saute, stirring until the onions are soft but not brown. Add all the vegetables except the peas and fry, stirring, for 5 minutes.

Add the water, cover and simmer over low heat for 20 minutes. Add the peas and simmer 5 minutes more. Most of the moisture should be absorbed during cooking.
Serves 4

RIBBON BEAN BAKE

1 tablespoon olive oil
1 onion, chopped
1 clove garlic, finely chopped
¼ cup chopped celery
1 tablespoon chilli sauce
½ cup tomato puree
¼ cup tomato paste
¼ cup red wine
freshly ground black pepper
¼ teaspoon dried oregano
¼ teaspoon dried basil
½ cup cooked butter beans
½ cup cooked red kidney beans
1 cup cooked soybeans
½ cup cooked lima beans
½ cup cooked chick peas
250 g ricotta cheese
250 g mozzarella cheese, thinly sliced
grated Parmesan cheese

Heat the oil and cook the onion, garlic and celery for 5 minutes. Add the chilli sauce, tomato puree and paste, wine, pepper, oregano and basil and simmer for 25 minutes.

Place all the beans and peas in a bowl and mix together. Beat the ricotta cheese in a bowl until smooth.

Place one-third of the tomato sauce in the bottom of a medium-sized casserole. Spoon in one-third of the bean mixture and spread one-third of the ricotta over the beans. Place one-third of the mozzarella slices on the ricotta.

Repeat layers twice and sprinkle the finished casserole with Parmesan cheese. Cover and bake at 190°C (375°F) for 30 minutes. Remove lid and bake for 10 minutes more to brown the top.
Serves 4-6

HUNGARIAN BEAN AND VEGETABLE LOAF

350 g borlotti beans
350 g soybeans
1 bay leaf
2 onions, finely chopped
4 cloves garlic, crushed
1 capsicum, seeded and diced
2 eggs, beaten
1 tablespoon oil
2 slices stale wholemeal bread,
   crumbed
1 tablespoon chopped fresh parsley
freshly ground black pepper
500 g spinach
100 g roasted unsalted peanuts
100 g button mushrooms
1-2 chillies, seeded and chopped
55 g can green peppercorns
1-2 tablespoons paprika

Soak the beans overnight in water to cover. Add the bay leaf, bring to the boil and simmer for 1 hour or until tender. Puree the beans in a blender with a little of the cooking liquid. Add the onions, garlic, capsicum, eggs, oil, breadcrumbs and parsley. Season to taste.

Remove the stalks from the spinach and cook in a little water until just tender. Puree the spinach and press out excess liquid between two plates. Puree the peanuts and mushrooms and add to the spinach with the chillies and green peppercorns.

Place the bean mixture on a floured board, flatten to a thickness of 4 cm with a rolling pin. Place the spinach mixture in the middle of the bean mixture and fold the bean mixture over to form a loaf. Sprinkle liberally with paprika then place it in a buttered ovenproof dish and bake at 190°C (375°F) for 1 hour. The loaf may be served hot or cold.
Serves 6-8

VEGETABLE KEBABS

Marinade
1 teaspoon garam masala
¼ teaspoon freshly ground black
   pepper
pinch dried rosemary
1 tablespoon cumin
3 tablespoons sesame oil
juice ½ lemon

Kebabs
4 button mushrooms
1 green or red capsicum, cut into
   squares
4 pickling onions
4 cherry tomatoes
½ eggplant, cut into 2.5 cm cubes
1 firm, ripe banana, cut into chunks
250 g tofu, cut into 2 cm cubes
4 spinach leaves, made into 2 cm thick
   rolls
4 cauliflower florets
1 apple, cut into cubes
continental parsley, for decoration

To make the marinade, place all the ingredients in a screw-top jar and shake well.

Arrange a selection of vegetables or fruit on skewers so that the cooking time of each is approximately the same. Brush over with the marinade and grill or bake on a barbecue. Garnish with continental parsley.
Serves 4

BARLEY VEGETABLE CASSEROLE

⅔ cup pearl barley
2½ cups chicken stock
1 tablespoon oil
1 clove garlic, crushed
1 onion, chopped
2 sticks celery, chopped
2 carrots, finely diced
2 tablespoons tomato paste
1 cup frozen peas

Soak the barley overnight in the stock. Bring to the boil and simmer for 1 hour. Drain the barley and reserve the liquid.

Heat the oil and saute the garlic, onion, celery and carrots for 8 minutes, stirring occasionally to prevent them from browning. Add the tomato paste, cook for 1 minute, then add the barley stock and the peas. Simmer for 20 minutes, until the vegetables are tender and the liquid has almost evaporated. Add the barley and reheat.
Serves 4

BAKED VEGETABLE RING WITH TOMATO FILLING

2 onions, chopped
2 cloves garlic, chopped
1 tablespoon oil
1 bunch spinach
2 cups cottage cheese
2 cups cooked soybeans
½ cup chopped walnuts
½ cup sultanas
¼ cup tomato paste
¼ cup grated carrot
¼ teaspoon dried dill
freshly ground black pepper

Fresh Tomato Filling
2 tomatoes, peeled and chopped
¼ cup chopped onion
1 tablespoon chopped fresh mint
1 tablespoon lemon juice
pinch cayenne pepper

Fry the onions and garlic in oil until they are soft but not brown. Wash the spinach and remove the stalks. Steam until just tender, then chop it finely and drain in a colander. When cool enough to handle, squeeze the spinach in your hands to remove all excess liquid. Combine the spinach with the cooked onion and all remaining ingredients.

Grease a ring tin and line it with greaseproof paper. Spoon in the spinach mixture and press down firmly. Cover the tin with foil and bake at 180°C (350°F) for 45 minutes or until firm when tested with your finger, removing the foil after 25 minutes. Allow to stand for 10 minutes before turning out onto a serving dish.

To make the filling, mix the tomatoes with all the remaining ingredients. Spoon into the centre of the vegetable ring and serve.
Serves 4–6

SOYARONI CHEESE

Soyaroni noodles can be substituted with homemade noodles or soybean noodles. To make soybean noodles combine 4 cups of soyflour, 2 egg yolks and 1 teaspoon of salt. Let the mixture sit for 15 minutes then roll out on a board to desired thickness. Cut into 36 cm strips, roll these lengthwise and then cut up the rolls into 1 cm pieces.

250 g Soyaroni noodles
40 g butter
2 tablespoons flour
1 teaspoon prepared mustard
3 cups milk
1½ cups grated Edam cheese
freshly ground black pepper
1 teaspoon chopped fresh dill
1 tablespoon chopped gherkins
1 cup soft breadcrumbs

Cook the noodles in boiling water until tender. Drain and rinse.

Melt the butter in a saucepan, stir in the flour and mustard and gradually add the milk. Stir constantly until the sauce thickens and boils, then reduce the heat and simmer for 3 minutes. Stir in 1 cup grated cheese, pepper, dill and gherkins.

Add the noodles and place in 4 individual ramekins. Mix the breadcrumbs with the remaining cheese and sprinkle over the top. Bake at 180°C (350°F) for 15 minutes, then place under the griller to brown before serving.
Serves 4

MAIN COURSES

Included here are recipes for fish, chicken and meat. It's not a very big chapter as the idea is to present some interesting, and for the most part, light, main courses. The recipes are not rigidly 'healthy' — there's even a recipe for deep-fried prawns and scallops — because following a healthy diet doesn't mean you have to miss out on all the things you enjoy. If you do that, you'll end up finding meal times a bore and going back to junk food.

So if you want to eat fried food occasionally, then do it, occasionally. The problems arise if you eat it every day, or every second or third day.

FISH PIE

350 g gemfish fillets
1½ cups milk
40 g butter
2 tablespoons flour
freshly ground black pepper
¼ cup finely chopped fresh parsley
1 hard-boiled egg, sliced
4 medium-sized potatoes, peeled
½ onion, thinly sliced
5 g butter
1 tablespoon hot milk
2 tablespoons grated Parmesan cheese

Place the fish and ½ cup of milk into an ovenproof dish. Cover and cook at 180°C (350°F) for 10–15 minutes. Remove the fish from the pan, flake it and discard bones. Reserve the milk.

In a saucepan, melt the butter and blend in the flour. Add the remaining milk plus the milk from the cooked fish, stir constantly and bring to the boil. Season with pepper and add the parsley. Return the fish to the casserole dish, add the sliced egg and pour over the sauce.

Steam the potatoes and onion together in a steamer for 20 minutes or until the potatoes are cooked. Then mash well with the 5 g butter and hot milk. Spread the mashed potato over the fish and sprinkle with cheese. Bake at 200°C (400°F) for 15 minutes.
Serves 2

PROVENCALE CHICKEN

8 chicken pieces
freshly ground black pepper
pinch cinnamon
¼ cup oil
1 clove garlic, crushed
1 bunch shallots, chopped
1 green capsicum, cut into strips
200 g button mushrooms
4 large tomatoes, peeled, seeded and chopped
120 mL dry white wine
150 mL tomato puree
bouquet garni
2 tablespoons fresh parsley, chopped
16 black olives

Season the chicken pieces with pepper and cinnamon. Heat the oil in a frying pan and brown the chicken pieces. Remove them with a slotted spoon and drain on paper towels.

Add the garlic, shallots, capsicum and mushrooms to the pan and saute. Remove and drain. Add the tomatoes to the pan and cook for 2–3 minutes, then add the wine.

Return the vegetables to the pan with the tomato puree, bouquet garni and chicken pieces. Cook over low heat until the chicken is tender. Serve garnished with parsley and olives.
Serves 4

APOLLO STEAK

4 sirloin or rump steaks
1 tablespoon oil

Sauce
25 g butter
1 large onion, sliced
1 lamb's kidney, skinned, cored and sliced
2 tomatoes, peeled, seeded and chopped
1 green capsicum, seeded and chopped
150 mL red wine
150 mL beef stock
pinch dried oregano

First make the sauce. Melt the butter in a saucepan and saute the onion for 5–8 minutes, until it is soft but not brown. Add the kidney, tomatoes and capsicum and simmer a further 5 minutes. Add the wine, stock and oregano, bring to the boil and simmer for 5 minutes.

Fry the steaks in oil until cooked to your taste. Spoon the sauce over and serve immediately.
Serves 4

EGGPLANT KHORESH

1 large eggplant, diced
salt
¾ cup haricot beans, soaked overnight
2 onions, sliced
2 carrots, sliced
1 tablespoon oil
1 kg best end neck of mutton, cut in chunks
½ cup flour
freshly ground black pepper
450 mL beef stock
1 tablespoon tomato paste
2 sticks celery, chopped

Put the diced eggplant in a colander and sprinkle with salt. Cover with a weighted plate and set aside for 30 minutes. The salt will draw out the eggplant's bitter juices.

Drain the beans. Fry the onions and carrots in the oil until the onion is soft but not brown. Remove with a slotted spoon.

Lightly coat the lamb in seasoned flour and brown in the oil remaining in the pan. Rinse and dry the eggplant and add it with the beans, onions and carrots, stock, tomato paste and celery. Bring to the boil, cover and simmer for 2½ hours or until the meat and beans are tender.

If possible, chill overnight or for several hours, until the fat has set on top. Remove the fat and reheat the dish before serving.
Serves 4–6

Stir-fried Chicken

GRILLED MARINATED FISH

2 thick snapper or bream fillets, cut in
  5 cm squares

Marinade
1 tablespoon vegetable oil
2 tablespoons fruit chutney
1 teaspoon grated fresh ginger
1 teaspoon soy sauce
1 tablespoon white wine

Mix together all the ingredients for the marinade.

Arrange the fish in a flat dish and pour over the marinade. Marinate for 2 hours, turning the fish once or twice during this time.

Line a grill pan with foil and arrange the fish pieces on it. Brush them with the marinade, using a pastry brush. Grill for 5 minutes, then brush with marinade again and grill a further 5 minutes or until the fish is cooked. It is not necessary to turn the fish.
Serves 2

CHICKEN HAWAIIAN

1½ cups pineapple juice
1 tablespoon finely chopped onion
1 teaspoon grated fresh ginger root
1 clove garlic, crushed
2 tablespoons fruit chutney
1 tablespoon soy sauce
1 kg chicken, cut in 4 pieces and
  skinned
fresh pineapple slices, to garnish

In a bowl, combine pineapple juice, onion, ginger, garlic, chutney and soy sauce to make a marinade.

Line a baking dish with foil and place the chicken pieces on it. Pour over the marinade and leave to marinate for 2 hours.

Bake the chicken in the marinade in an oven preheated to 190°C (375°F) for three-quarters of an hour. Baste from time to time. When chicken is cooked, remove and serve with fresh pineapple slices.
Serves 4

BAKED FISH CASSEROLE

250 g frozen white fish, cut in 2
2 tablespoons lemon juice
freshly ground black pepper
1 tablespoon finely chopped fresh
  parsley
½ onion, thinly sliced
pinch dried dill
2 tablespoons dry breadcrumbs
1 tablespoon vegetable oil

Place frozen fish in a baking dish. Pour over lemon juice, grate some pepper and cover with parsley, onion slices and a pinch of dill. Bake in an oven preheated to 190°C (375°F) for 15 minutes.

Mix breadcrumbs and oil together and spread lightly over your casserole. Brown in the oven for 5 minutes.
Serves 2

STIR-FRIED CHICKEN

2 teaspoons soy sauce
4 chicken breasts, cut into strips
2 tablespoons oil
1 large onion, quartered
1 teaspoon grated ginger root
1 clove garlic, crushed
2 sticks celery, sliced diagonally
1 red capsicum, sliced
1 small carrot, sliced
285 g can baby corn, drained
4 cups button mushrooms
2 teaspoons cornflour
200 mL chicken stock
4 shallots, chopped

Sprinkle soy sauce over the chicken strips. Heat the oil in a wok and gently fry the chicken until cooked. Remove with a slotted spoon and drain. Add onion, ginger, garlic and celery to the wok and stir-fry over high heat. Add capsicum, carrot and corn and stir-fry. Lower the heat and add the button mushrooms.

Blend the cornflour with the stock and add to the wok with the chicken pieces and shallots. Increase the heat, stirring constantly, and cook until heated through.
Serves 6

LAMB AND NUT KORMA

50 g raw, unsalted cashew nuts
3 dried chillies
2 teaspoons ground coriander
1 teaspoon ground ginger
1 teaspoon ground cumin
½ teaspoon cinnamon
pinch ground cardamon
pinch ground cloves
2 cloves garlic, crushed
150 mL water
3 onions, chopped
50 g butter or ghee
150 ml natural yoghurt
750 g lean lamb, diced
grated rind ½ lemon
2 teaspoons lemon juice
½ teaspoon turmeric

Grind the nuts and chillies together. If using a food processor, a little water may be needed. Mix together the coriander, ginger, cumin, cinnamon, cardamon, cloves and garlic. Add the nut mixture and water and blend to a smooth paste.

Fry the onions in the butter over low heat until they are soft but not brown. Stir in the spice and nut paste and add the yoghurt. Fry over gentle heat until the oil separates.

Add the lamb, toss well in the mixture and add the lemon rind and juice and the turmeric. Bring to the boil, cover and simmer for 1 hour.
Serves 4

GEMFISH WITH PEANUT SAUCE

1 kg gemfish fillets, skinned
2 tablespoons flour
2 tablespoons oil
25 g butter
2 tablespoons smooth peanut butter
1 tablespoon honey
1 tablespoon soy sauce
1 tablespoon vinegar
150 mL flat light beer
pinch chilli powder
½ cup raw unsalted peanuts
1 lemon, cut into wedges

Divide the fish into 4 pieces. Coat each piece lightly with flour. Heat the oil and butter together and fry the fish for 5 minutes on each side.

Place all the remaining ingredients except the peanuts and lemon wedges in a pan and boil until the mixture has reduced by half. Add the peanuts and simmer over low heat for 3 minutes.

Put the fish on a heated serving dish and spoon the sauce over. Serve with lemon wedges.
Serves 4

CURRIED FISH RISOTTO

1 large onion, chopped
2 tablespoons oil
1 tablespoon flour
1–2 tablespoons curry powder
550 mL chicken stock
1 cup long-grain rice
1 green capsicum, sliced
1 small Granny Smith apple, peeled, cored and chopped
1 tablespoon sultanas
freshly ground black pepper
750 g white fish, skinned and boned

Saute the onion in the oil until soft but not brown. Stir in the flour and curry powder and cook for 1 minute. Add the stock, rice, capsicum, apple and sultanas and season to taste. Cover the pan and simmer for 15 minutes, stirring occasionally.

Cut the fish into bite-sized pieces, add to the curry and simmer for 5 minutes, until rice and fish are cooked.
Serves 4

CHICKEN CHASSEUR

½ chicken, cut into 4 pieces
freshly ground black pepper
½ onion, chopped
½ apple, chopped
115 g fresh mushrooms, sliced
1 clove garlic, chopped
½ cup white wine
1 cup commercial tomato sauce for pasta (e.g. Alora, Pomarola)

Remove the skin from the chicken pieces and place the chicken in a casserole. Sprinkle with pepper and brown in a 200°C (400°F) oven for 10 minutes. Spoon off fat carefully, and arrange onion, apple, mushrooms and garlic around chicken. Pour in wine and tomato sauce and bake at 180°C (350°F) for 40 minutes.
Serves 2

SPICY PEANUT ROAST CHICKEN

1 teaspoon paprika
1 teaspoon ground ginger
pinch cayenne pepper
3 tablespoons oil
3 cups raw unsalted peanuts
1.5 kg chicken
125 g butter
3–4 slices wholemeal bread
2 tablespoons rum

Mix paprika, ginger, cayenne and oil together. Grind 1 cup peanuts in a food processor and add half of it to the oil and spice mixture. Use it to coat the chicken all over. Bake the chicken at 180°C (350°F) for 1½ hours or until tender.

Mix the remaining ground peanuts with half the butter. Toast the bread, spread it with the peanut butter, place on a baking sheet and bake for 5–10 minutes, or until the topping is brown and bubbling.

Fry the remaining peanuts in the rest of the butter until they are pale golden.

To serve, cut the toast in half and arrange around the chicken on a hot serving dish. Sprinkle the peanuts over, heat the rum carefully, pour it over the chicken and set alight.
Serves 6

STEAMED TROUT WITH LIME BUTTER

2 small fresh trout, washed and dried
juice 2 limes
pinch of *herbes de Provence* (dried
   thyme, rosemary, marjoram and
   oregano)
freshly ground black pepper

Lime Butter
4 tablespoons butter
grated rind and juice ½ lime

To make the lime butter, beat the butter
with a wooden spoon or in a food
processor until smooth. Beat in rind and
juice thoroughly, then transfer to a dec-
orative serving bowl and refrigerate
until needed.
   Cut out two 30 cm (12 inch) squares of
aluminium foil. Arrange each trout on
the foil and place 1 teaspoon of lime butter inside each fish. Squeeze lime juice
over, sprinkle on seasoning and cook in
a steamer for 15 minutes. Serve with
remaining lime butter.
Serves 2

BARRAMUNDI KEBABS

4 pickling onions, peeled
250 g barramundi or gemfish fillets, cut
   in 2.5 cm squares
6 button mushrooms
½ red capsicum, cut into pieces

Marinade
1 tablespoon vegetable oil
pinch dried thyme
pinch dried marjoram
½ cup lemon juice
2 bay leaves
½ teaspoon chopped fresh parsley

Mix together, in a large shallow bowl,
all the ingredients for the marinade.
   Cook the onions whole in water for 15
minutes. Thread the fish squares on
skewers alternately with small onions,
mushrooms and pieces of capsicum.
   Put the fish kebabs in the marinade
and leave for 1 hour, turning often.
Grill for 10–15 minutes, turning fre-
quently to cook all over: alternatively,
cook on a barbecue.
Serves 2

Steamed Trout with Lime Butter

DEEP-FRIED SCALLOPS AND PRAWNS

20 scallops
20 uncooked king prawns
. cup white wine
. cup water
bouquet garni
freshly ground black pepper
wholemeal flour
oil for deep-frying
lime wedges

Batter
. cup wholemeal flour
. cup milk
. egg, separated
pinch cayenne pepper

Tartare Sauce
. cup mayonnaise
. teaspoon capers, finely chopped
. teaspoon chopped chives
. teaspoon French mustard

To make the batter, sift the flour and blend in the milk, egg yolk and cayenne pepper. Set aside to rest for 20 minutes. Beat the egg white until stiff and fold it into the batter.
To make the tartare sauce, whisk together all the ingredients.
Clean the scallops and peel and devein the prawns. Heat the wine with the water and bouquet garni. Blanch the seafood in the liquid, remove and drain. Season the seafood, coat with flour and dip into batter. Deep-fry each piece until golden and drain. Serve hot with tartare sauce and lime wedges.
Serves 4

BAKED CHICKEN ORIENTAL

1 kg chicken
½ green capsicum, cut in strips
½ red capsicum, cut in strips

Sauce
1 cup pineapple pieces in natural juice
2 tablespoons cornflour
1 tablespoon sugar
¼ cup cider vinegar
2 tablespoons fruit chutney
1 teaspoon grated fresh ginger root
1 teaspoon soy sauce

Put all the sauce ingredients into a saucepan, bring to the boil, and cook, stirring until thick. Pour it over the chicken in a baking dish.
Bake at 180°C (350°F) for 30 minutes. Add the capsicum strips and bake, uncovered for 15 minutes longer or until the chicken is cooked.
Serves 4

CHICKEN FILLETS WITH TOMATO TOPPING

2 chicken fillets, skin removed
1 tomato, chopped
½ small white onion, sliced thinly
1 teaspoon chopped fresh tarragon
½ teaspoon dried thyme
½ clove garlic, crushed
freshly ground black pepper
2 teaspoons butter, softened

Cut out two 30 cm (12 inch) squares of foil. Place one chicken fillet on each square.
Mix together in a bowl, the tomato, onion, tarragon, thyme, garlic, pepper and butter. Place half of this mixture on top of each chicken fillet. Fold up the foil and seal. Steam for 20 minutes and serve in the foil.
Serves 2

GRILLED KINGFISH CUTLETS

4 whole kingfish cutlets
1 teaspoon French mustard
juice 1 lemon
freshly ground black pepper
40 g butter
coriander flowers, to garnish

Heat the griller. Smear mustard onto the cutlets. Place the fish on foil, sprinkle with lemon juice, season lightly and dot with knobs of butter.
Grill until fish flakes when tested. Serve garnished with coriander flowers.
Serves 4

FISH A LA GRECQUE

2 large potatoes, peeled and sliced
1 onion, chopped
250 g fish fillets
2 large tomatoes, sliced
½ cup water
2 tablespoons vegetable oil
freshly ground black pepper
½ cup finely chopped fresh parsley

Lay the potato slices on the bottom of a casserole dish and sprinkle with chopped onion. Place a layer of fish fillets on top and cover with sliced tomato. Pour over the water and oil and sprinkle with pepper and parsley. Bake at 150°C (300°F) for 30 minutes.
Serves 2

FISH FLORENTINE

225 g white fish fillets
½ cup water
⅓ cup lemon juice
1 bay leaf
1 shallot, finely chopped
1 stick celery, quartered
1 bunch spinach, cooked
2 tablespoons grated Cheddar cheese
red capsicum, to garnish

Put the fish into a pan and add the water, lemon juice, bay leaf, shallot and celery. Cover the pan and simmer for about 10 minutes or until the fish is tender.
Drain the spinach and place in the bottom of an ovenproof casserole dish. Arrange the cooked fish over it, sprinkle with cheese and grill until the cheese has melted. Serve decorated with red capsicum.
Serves 2

CHICKEN AND VEGETABLE STIR-FRY

2 tablespoons vegetable oil
2 skinned chicken fillets, cut in bite-sized pieces
½ red capsicum, cut in thin strips
½ green capsicum, cut in thin strips
1 carrot, cut in thin strips
8 green beans, sliced
2 shallots, sliced
¼ cup sliced almonds, toasted

Sauce
1 cup pineapple juice
2 tablespoons fruit chutney
1 tablespoon soy sauce
½ teaspoon grated fresh ginger root
2 teaspoons cornflour

Mix together all the sauce ingredients and set aside.
Heat the oil in a frying pan and add the chicken pieces. Stir-fry for about 3 minutes, or until cooked. Steam the capsicums, carrots, beans and shallots for 5 minutes in a steamer.
Add the sauce to the chicken in the pan. Heat, stirring until the sauce thickens. Add the hot steamed vegetables and almonds, mix well and serve with brown rice.
Serves 2

Deep-fried Scallops and Prawns (above)
and Fish Florentine

Sesame Grilled Chicken

SPICY CHICKEN FILLETS

2 chicken fillets, skin removed
½ red capsicum, cut into thin strips
½ green capsicum, cut into thin strips

Topping
1 teaspoon grated fresh ginger root
½ clove garlic, crushed
½ cup mango chutney
pinch cayenne pepper
2 teaspoons butter, softened

Mix the topping ingredients together in a bowl and set aside.

Cut out two 30 cm (12 inch) squares of foil and place a chicken fillet on each one. Place half the topping mixture on each chicken fillet and cover each one with half the capsicum strips.

Fold up the foil into a parcel and seal. Steam for 20 minutes and serve in the foil.
Serves 2

SEAFOOD PASTA

24 mussels, well washed and scraped
1 cup dry white wine
225 g sliced mushrooms
12 shallots, finely sliced
50 g butter
500 g large peeled uncooked prawns
bouquet garni
¼ teaspoon paprika
1 tablespoon brandy (optional)
225 g pasta
150 mL fresh or canned tomato puree
finely chopped fresh parsley

Place mussels in a large pan with the wine, cover the pan and cook over high heat until the shells open. Remove the mussels with a slotted spoon, strain the liquid and reserve. Remove most of the mussels from their shells, reserving a few for garnish.

Cook the mushrooms and shallots in the butter for 3 minutes then add the prawns, bouquet garni and paprika. Cook for a minute or two, add brandy if using, and flame. Douse the flames with the reserved mussel liquid and simmer for a few minutes more. Remove the prawns and reduce the liquid in the pan by half.

Boil the pasta until tender and drain. Add tomato sauce to the mussel liquid and bring to the boil. Add mussels and prawns and cook just until they are heated through. Remove bouquet garni. Put the pasta into a warmed serving plate, spoon the sauce over the top, decorate with reserved mussels in their shells and lots of chopped parsley.
Serves 4-6

SESAME GRILLED CHICKEN

2 chicken fillets, washed, dried and
    skinned
2 tablespoons sesame seeds

Marinade
½ carrot, chopped
½ onion, chopped
pinch ground cloves
6 peppercorns
1 tablespoon chopped fresh parsley
½ teaspoon dried thyme
2 tablespoons vegetable oil
3 teaspoons lemon juice
¼ cup white wine

In a bowl, mix together all the marinade ingredients.

Arrange the chicken fillets on a flat dish and pour the marinade over them. Leave to marinate for at least 1 hour. Preheat the grill to high. Place the chicken on foil, brush with the marinade and grill for 5 minutes. Turn and brush with more marinade and grill for a further 5 minutes or until the chicken is cooked. Turn off the grill, brush the chicken with more marinade, shake sesame seeds over and leave under the turned-off grill for a few minutes before serving. Slice chicken fillet. Serve with rice.
Serves 2

VEAL PARMIGIANA

4 large veal scallops
freshly ground black pepper
1 cup flour, sifted
½ teaspoon dried oregano
2 eggs, beaten
½ cup grated Parmesan cheese
1½ cups breadcrumbs
oil, for frying
1 cup grated mozzarella cheese
2 cups tomato sauce, fresh or canned
fresh oregano, to garnish

Flatten the scallops with a meat mallet, season and coat with flour. In a shallow bowl, mix together the oregano and eggs and in another bowl, combine the Parmesan with the breadcrumbs.

Dip each scallop into egg and coat with breadcrumbs. Heat the oil and fry each scallop over high heat for 1 minute on each side. Remove from the pan and place in a shallow casserole dish. Sprinkle each scallop with grated mozzarella and pour over the tomato sauce.

Bake at 180°C (350°F) for 10 minutes or until the cheese has melted. Serve garnished with oregano.
Serves 4

Seafood Pasta (above) and Veal Parmigiana

FISH PROVENCALE

350 g gemfish fillets
⅓ cup lemon juice
freshly ground black pepper
1 clove garlic, crushed
2 tomatoes, peeled and sliced
¼ cup finely chopped fresh parsley
⅓ cup dry white wine
1 tablespoon chopped fresh basil
1 teaspoon *herbes de Provence* (dried
  thyme, rosemary, marjoram and
  oregano)
¼ cup pine nuts

Sprinkle fish with lemon juice and pepper, then grill for 15 minutes until fish is well cooked.

In a frying pan, place garlic, tomatoes, parsley, wine and basil. Bring to the boil, reduce heat and cook for 15 minutes. When the mixture has slightly thickened, pour it over fish, sprinkle on herbs and pine nuts, and serve.
Serves 2

BEEF COBBLER

750 g chuck steak, diced
¼ cup oil
1 onion, chopped
1 carrot, chopped
4 tablespoons flour
1 tablespoon tomato paste
300 mL beef stock
300 mL beer
1 clove garlic, crushed
pinch dried rosemary
1 tablespoon milk
1 tablespoon chopped fresh parsley

Brown the steak in the oil, add the onion and carrot and cook for 5 minutes. Stir in the flour and cook for 1 minute. Add all the remaining ingredients and bring to the boil.

Transfer to an ovenproof dish, cover and bake at 150°C (300°F) for 2 hours, or until the beef is tender.
Serves 6

CURRIED CHICKEN

1 Granny Smith apple, peeled and
  sliced
1 onion, very finely chopped
1½ cups apple juice
2 tablespoons mango chutney
2 teaspoons curry powder
1 tablespoon flour
2 cups cooked chicken, cut into bite-
  sized pieces
1 banana, chopped
1 cup pineapple pieces
blanched almonds to garnish

Put the apple and onion into a saucepan with the apple juice and cook over low heat until the onion is soft. Add the mango chutney.

Blend the curry powder and flour together and make a paste with a little water. Add to the apple mixture and stir until thickened.

Just before serving, add the chicken pieces and heat through. Do not stir too much. Add the banana and pineapple pieces and serve garnished with blanched almonds. Serve with rice.
Serves 4

JEWISH FISH BALLS

500 g white fish fillets
1 egg, beaten
75 g medium matzo meal
1 small onion, finely chopped
freshly ground black pepper
flour, for dusting
250 g carrots, thinly sliced
450 mL fish stock
1 bay leaf

Mince or puree the fish and combine with the egg, matzo meal and onion and season to taste. Roll the mixture into 12 balls, using floured hands.

Arrange the carrots and fish balls in a shallow ovenproof dish, pour over the stock and add the bay leaf. Cover and bake at 180°C (350°F) for 1 hour. Remove the bay leaf before serving.
Serves 4

TROUT IN FOIL

2 small fresh trout, washed and dried
2 teaspoons butter
1 teaspoon lemon juice
1 teaspoon chopped fresh mint

Mix the butter with the lemon juice and mint. Place half of this mixture into the cavity of each trout.

Cut out two 30 cm (12 inch) squares of foil and place a trout on each one. Wrap securely and steam for 15 minutes. Serve in the foil with lemon wedges.
Serves 2

ORANGE CHICKEN PARCELS

2 chicken fillets, skin removed
1 tablespoon vegetable oil
1 small apple, thinly sliced
juice ½ orange
orange rind, to garnish
shallots to garnish

Heat the oil in a pan and brown the chicken fillets on both sides. Cut out two 30 cm (12 inch) squares of foil and place a chicken fillet on each one. Arrange sliced apple on top of the chicken and squeeze over the orange juice. Seal the parcel and steam for 20 minutes. Serve in the foil garnished with julienned orange rind and shallots.
Serves 2

FISH IN FOIL PACKETS

2 teaspoons oil
4 white fish fillets
½ teaspoon grated lemon rind
2 tablespoons lemon juice
2 tablespoons finely chopped parsley
1 teaspoon chopped fresh dill
1 tablespoon chopped fresh chives
freshly ground black pepper
½ teaspoon soy sauce

Cut out two 30 cm (12 inch) square pieces of foil and lightly brush them with oil. Place 2 fish fillets on each square.

Mix together in a bowl, the lemon rind and juice, herbs, pepper and soy sauce. Spread half of this mixture over the fish in each foil square. Wrap up the parcel and steam for 15 minutes. Serve in the foil.
Serves 2

Orange Chicken Parcels

ACCOMPANIMENTS

Many of these vegetable dishes will also make fine first courses. Some, like Souffle Potatoes will make a light meal, served with a salad. Most of the time you'll probably serve your vegetables simply boiled or steamed, but every now and again it's nice to give them a special lift by cooking them in a different way. This is especially true of potatoes, which are the most versatile of vegetables, so there are more potato dishes included than any other vegetable.

BROCCOLI IN CAPER SAUCE

500 g broccoli
1 cup buttermilk
2 tablespoons cornflour
1 cup yoghurt
freshly ground black pepper
2 teaspoons chopped capers
½ teaspoon turmeric
4 tablespoons sour cream

Trim broccoli stalks and slit from base to flower. Peel the stalks if they look woody. Stand the stalks in boiling salted water with the flower heads above the water and cook for about 8 minutes, until the stalks are just tender. Drain and cover to keep warm while preparing the sauce.

Blend the buttermilk with the cornflour and heat in a saucepan, stirring occasionally. Add the yoghurt, pepper, capers and turmeric, stirring until the sauce thickens. Add the sour cream and heat through without boiling.

Place broccoli on a serving dish, spoon some sauce over and serve the remainder separately.
Serves 4

SOUFFLE POTATOES

4 large old potatoes
1 cup grated Cheddar cheese
freshly ground black pepper
4 tablespoons sour cream
1 tablespoon chopped chives
1 tablespooon chopped fresh parsley
pinch paprika
2 egg yolks
3 egg whites

Wash the potatoes, pierce with a skewer in several places and bake at 180°C (350°F) for 1-1½ hours. The potatoes should be cooked but still intact. Cut a lid off each potato and scoop out the centre, leaving some of the flesh around the skin to form a casing.

Mash the potato with all the remaining ingredients except the egg whites. Beat the egg whites until stiff and gently fold into the potato mixture. Spoon into potato cases and place them on an oven tray. Bake at 200°C (400°F) until the tops are golden brown and puffy.
Serves 4

GLAZED ONIONS

18 small white onions, peeled
40 g butter
1 tablespoon olive oil
freshly ground black pepper
1 bay leaf
½ cup chicken stock
2 tablespoons white vermouth
2 tablespoons chopped fresh parsley

Cut a cross in the root end of each onion to prevent the centres from falling out. Brown them in butter and oil. Season with pepper.

Place onions with their cooking butter into a baking dish. Add bay leaf, chicken stock and vermouth.

Cover and bake in a 180°C (350°F) oven for 1 hour. Turn onions every 20 minutes. Garnish with parsley to serve.
Serves 6

DHAL

500 g green lentils
1-2 tablespoons ghee or oil
2-3 onions, finely sliced
2-3 tomatoes, peeled and chopped
1 teaspoon chilli powder
2 teaspoons turmeric
salt
2 tablespoons tomato paste

Soak the lentils in water to cover for 30 minutes. Heat the ghee and saute the onions until they are soft but not brown. Add tomatoes, chilli powder, turmeric and salt. Cook, stirring, for 5 minutes.

Drain the lentils and put them in a pan with enough water to cover. Bring to the boil, add the onion mixture and simmer for 1 hour until thick and mushy. Stir in tomato paste and serve with rice or curried vegetables.
Serves 6

POTATO CROQUETTES

1 tablespoon milk
20 g butter
2 egg yolks
500 g mashed potatoes
freshly ground black pepper
1 tablespoon chopped fresh parsley
1 egg, whisked
breadcrumbs
oil, for deep-frying

Heat the milk in a pan and add the butter. Off the heat, stir until the butter has melted. Stir in egg yolks. Beat in mashed potatoes, pepper and parsley. Divide into portions and shape into croquettes.

Dip first in whisked egg and then roll in breadcrumbs. Deep-fry in hot oil until brown. Drain on kitchen paper before serving. The croquettes may be kept warm in a low oven or even reheated on another occasion.
Serves 4-6

FENNEL SAUTE

3 heads fennel
60 g butter
freshly ground black pepper
grated rind ½ lemon
juice ½ lemon
1 tablespoon chopped fresh parsley
fresh chives, to garnish

Wash fennel and cut into thin slices from top to bottom. Melt the butter in a pan, add the fennel, cover and cook for 5 minutes. Remove the lid and cook for a further 5 minutes. Transfer to a serving dish and keep it warm.

Add all the remaining ingredients to the pan, heat through and pour over the fennel. Serve garnished with chives.
Serves 4

BAKED TURNIPS

2 turnips, peeled and diced
½ cup chicken stock
4 tablespoons dark honey

Preheat the oven to 180°C (350°F) and place turnips in a buttered casserole dish.

Mix warm stock with honey and pour it over the turnips. Cover the dish and bake for 45 minutes or until tender.
Serves 4

PARSNIPS WITH HERBS

6 parsnips
90 g butter
juice 1 lemon
freshly ground black pepper
1 cup chicken stock
1 tablespoon finely chopped fresh herbs
   (parsley, chives, dill, marjoram)
fresh thyme, for decoration

Peel parsnips thinly and cut them into large matchsticks. Put the butter, lemon juice, pepper and stock into a frying pan and bring to the boil. Add the parsnips and herbs and cook, uncovered, until the stock has reduced and the parsnips are tender. Add more stock if necessary. Garnish with thyme.
Serves 4

Pages 76–77: Clockwise from top left: Fennel Saute, Orange Glazed Carrots, Braised Broad Beans, Baby Squash with Dill, Glazed Brussels Sprouts and Parsnips with Herbs

BABY SQUASH WITH DILL

500 g miniature squash, topped and
   tailed
60 g butter
1 cup water
freshly ground black pepper
1 tablespoon finely chopped fresh dill
juice ½ lemon
fresh dill, to garnish

Place squash in a heavy saucepan with butter and water. Season with pepper. Cover the pan and bring to the boil, then reduce heat and simmer for 5 minutes.

Add dill and lemon juice, and let it boil, uncovered, until the liquid has almost evaporated. Serve immediately garnished with dill.
Serves 4–6

ORANGE GLAZED CARROTS

125 g butter
juice 2 oranges
¼ cup brown sugar
500 g carrots, cut into sticks
¼ teaspoon cinnamon
fresh basil, to garnish

Melt the butter in a deep frying pan. Stir in the orange juice and sugar and bring to the boil. Lower the heat and cook for 3 minutes, stirring constantly.

Add the carrots, sprinkle with cinnamon and cook, stirring from time to time, until the juice has almost evaporated and the carrots are tender. Decorate with basil.
Serves 6

GLAZED BRUSSELS SPROUTS

1 kg Brussels sprouts
1½ cups chicken stock
10 tablespoons honey
pinch ground cloves
1 tablespoon lemon juice
fresh sage, to garnish

Cut the stalks of the Brussels sprouts level with the base and cut a cross into the base. Bring a pan of water to the boil and blanch the sprouts briefly. Drain and place in a heavy saucepan. Barely cover with chicken stock and add honey and cloves. Cook until just tender. Remove sprouts and keep warm while reducing liquid by boiling briskly. When liquid has halved in quantity, add lemon juice, pour mixture over sprouts and serve garnished with sage.
Serves 6–8

POTATO STICKS

250 g potatoes
2 egg yolks
60 g butter
125 g plain flour
freshly ground black pepper
1 tablespoon chopped chives
1 egg, beaten

Peel the potatoes and cook in boiling salted water until tender. Drain and mash with the egg yolks and butter until creamy. Add the flour, pepper and

chives and mix well. Form the dough
into a round shape and chill for 30
minutes.

Roll it out into a rectangle 1 cm thick.
Cut into sticks 1 cm wide and 6 cm long.
Twist and brush lightly with beaten egg.

Place on a greased oven tray and
bake at 200°C (400°F) for 10 minutes or
until golden brown and crisp. Leave on
the tray until they are cool.
Makes 40

BRAISED BROAD
BEANS

500 g broad beans in their pods
4 tablespoons oil
1 onion, chopped
1 clove garlic, crushed
1 tablespoon chopped fresh parsley
1 tablespoon chopped fresh dill
freshly ground black pepper
pinch nutmeg
1 cup water mixed with 1 tablespoon
    tomato puree

Shell beans. Heat the oil in a saucepan,
add the beans, onion and garlic and
cook over moderate heat, stirring, for 2
minutes. Add the remaining ingredients
and bring to the boil.

Add enough water to keep the mixture from frying and cover the pan.
Cook for 25 minutes, adding more water
if necessary.
Serves 6

Baked Turnips (left) and Potato Sticks

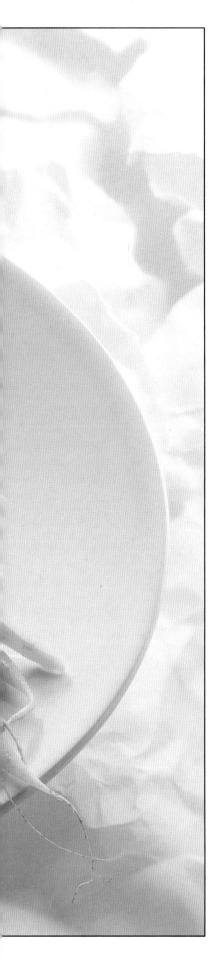

BABY CARROTS WITH FRESH BASIL

500 g baby carrots
2 tablespoons finely chopped fresh basil
40 g butter

Place carrots in a saucepan and just cover with boiling water. Cover the pan, bring to the boil and cook for 10 minutes. Drain, toss well with basil, add butter and return to the heat. Allow the butter to melt, mixing well with the carrots.
Serves 6

FINNISH HASSELBACK POTATOES

12 potatoes, peeled
1 teaspoon salt
60 g butter
4 tablespoons grated Parmesan cheese
2 tablespoons breadcrumbs

Cut potatoes into thin slices but not quite through to the lower edge, so that the slices hold together.

Place potatoes, with slices up, into a well-buttered casserole. Sprinkle with salt and dot with butter. Bake at 230°C (450°F) for 20 minutes, basting occasionally with the melted butter. Sprinkle with cheese and breadcrumbs and bake for another 25 minutes without basting.
Serves 6

RATATOUILLE

½ small eggplant, sliced and cut in 4
1 zucchini, sliced
1 carrot, sliced
¼ red capsicum, sliced
¼ green capsicum, sliced
1 onion, peeled and sliced
1 clove garlic, finely chopped
3 tomatoes, roughly chopped
1 tablespoon chopped fresh basil

Place all the ingredients in a nonstick frying pan and cook gently for 30 minutes. Stir from time to time to prevent sticking.
Serves 2

Baby Carrots with Fresh Basil

SWEET POTATOES WITH PINEAPPLE IN FOIL

1 large sweet potato, peeled and sliced in 1 cm thick slices
4 tablespoons pineapple, chopped
2 teaspoons margarine

Orange and Ginger Sauce
2 tablespoons cornflour
1 cup orange juice
1 tablespoon margarine
1 teaspoon orange rind, grated
½ teaspoon ground ginger

Cut out 2 sheets of foil about 30.5 cm (12 inches) square. On each foil sheet, place half the sweet potato slices topped with pineapple and margarine. Wrap and seal in the foil, place in a steamer and cook for 20 minutes. Serve with sauce.

To make sauce, in a pan blend cornflour with a little orange juice. Add remaining juice, margarine, grated orange rind and ginger, and thicken over gentle heat.
Serves 2

MEXICAN SUCCOTASH

½ red capsicum, cut into 1.5 cm squares
½ green capsicum, cut into 1.5 cm squares
4 small white onions, halved
½ cup peas
½ cup corn kernels
½ cup fresh lima beans
1 tablespoon oil
1 tablespoon chopped fresh basil
fresh basil or parsley, to garnish

Place all the vegetables in a steamer and cook for 10 minutes.

In a pan, heat oil and stir vegetables around for several minutes. Add basil and serve with fresh herbs.
Serves 2

STRING BEANS WITH ALMONDS

500 g string beans, sliced
4 tablespoons toasted, slivered almonds
butter, to serve

Place beans and almonds in a steamer. Secure lid and steam for 6 minutes. Serve with dobs of butter.
Serves 4

FRUIT AND DESSERTS

The healthiest and usually the most delicious dessert is fresh fruit in season. Strawberries in spring and summer, summer stone fruit, summer tropical fruit, pears and oranges in winter. There's a chart on pages 18–19 showing some of the new tropical fruit available and how to prepare and eat it.

However, sometimes we all have a craving for dessert. In winter especially, a dried fruit crumble or a rice dish is comforting and warming. And when, at the end of the season we've had enough of fresh strawberries, a strawberry sorbet makes a delicious change. Most of the recipes here are based on fruit and they're all very simple to prepare.

ORANGE AND RHUBARB COMPOTE

1 bunch rhubarb
2 oranges
½ cup brown sugar
¼ cup water

Wash the rhubarb and trim the stalks. Cut into 3 cm lengths. Peel the oranges, making sure all the pith is removed. Cut into thin rounds and remove all pips.

Layer the fruit in a baking dish and sprinkle with sugar. Add water and bake at 185°C (360°F) until the rhubarb is tender. Serve hot or cold.
Serves 4

POACHED PEACHES

4 fresh peaches
¼ cup flaked coconut
¼ cup ground almonds
½ teaspoon finely grated orange rind
1 egg yolk
40 g butter
1 cup white wine
1 cinnamon stick

Plunge the peaches into boiling water and leave for 1 minute. Drain, cover with cold water and peel the peaches. Slice the peaches and remove the stones.

Mix together the coconut, almonds, orange rind and egg yolk and spoon in between the peach slices. Dot with butter, pour wine around the peaches and add the cinnamon stick. Cover and bake at 180°C (350°F) for 20 minutes or until the peaches are tender. Remove the cinnamon stick and serve warm with custard.
Serves 4

KISSEL

2 cups blackberries
1 lemon, juiced
¼ cup honey
⅛ teaspoon powdered cinnamon
2 cups water
1½ tablespoons arrowroot
1½ tablespoons potato flour
150 mL yoghurt or sour cream

Place blackberries, lemon juice, honey, cinnamon in 1¼ cups water and boil for 5 minutes. Strain through sieve or puree in blender. Return mixture to pan and bring back to boil.

Mix arrowroot and potato flour with remaining water and add to blackberry puree. Cook 4 minutes then pour into individual dishes and cool. Serve topped with yoghurt or sour cream.
Serves 4

PINEAPPLE CALYPSO

1 ripe pineapple
6 tablespoons chopped fresh mint
2 egg whites
½ cup caster sugar

Peel the pineapple and cut it into quarters lengthways. Remove the hard core from the centre of each quarter and cut the pineapple into small cubes. Mix with the chopped mint and chill overnight.

Spoon the pineapple into heatproof serving bowls. Beat the egg whites until stiff and add half the sugar, beating until dissolved. Beat in the remaining sugar and spoon over the pineapple. Place under a griller to brown the meringue.
Serves 4

GINGER SOUFFLE

60 g butter
3 tablespoons plain flour
1½ cups milk
2 tablespoons sugar
3 eggs, separated
1 teaspoon vanilla essence
2 teaspoons grated ginger in syrup
icing sugar

Melt the butter in a saucepan, stir in the flour and cook for 1 minute. Add the milk gradually, stirring constantly, to form a smooth sauce. Add the sugar and stir until it has dissolved. Cool the sauce slightly.

Beat the egg yolks into the sauce with the vanilla essence and ginger. Beat the egg whites until stiff and fold them into the sauce. Spoon the mixture into a souffle dish and bake at 190°C (375°F) for 40 minutes. Sprinkle with sieved icing sugar and serve immediately.
Serves 4–6

Chinese Pears

APRICOT MOUSSE

500 g ripe apricots
juice ½ lemon
3 tablespoons icing sugar
2 teaspoons gelatine
¼ cup cold water
½ cup cream
whipped cream (optional)
mint leaves, to garnish

Plunge the apricots into boiling water and leave for 1 minute. Drain, cover with cold water and peel. Cut the apricots in half and remove stones. Puree the apricots with lemon juice and icing sugar in a blender or sieve.

Place the gelatine in the water and stand over a bowl of hot water until dissolved. Stir it into the apricot puree.

Beat the cream until stiff and fold into the apricot mixture. Spoon into individual serving dishes and chill until set. Serve with whipped cream garnished with mint leaves.
Serves 4

DRIED FRUIT CRUMBLE

1 cup dried apricots
1 cup dried figs
1 cup pitted prunes
¼ cup raisins
¼ cup currants
¼ cup sugar
1 cup water
¼ cup almonds
2 tablespoons flour
¼ cup desiccated coconut
¼ cup brown sugar
40 g butter

Soak the fruit for 1 hour in enough water to cover, then drain. Place the sugar and water in a saucepan and bring to the boil. Add the fruit and simmer for 30 minutes or until the liquid has been absorbed. Add the almonds and place the mixture in an ovenproof serving dish.

Combine all the remaining ingredients and sprinkle over the fruit. Bake at 200°C (400°F) for 15–20 minutes or until the top is golden.
Serves 4-6

CHINESE PEARS

4 ripe pears
1 litre water
½ cup sugar
1 cinnamon stick
4 cloves
3 tablespoons chopped walnuts
3 tablespoons chopped dates
¼ cup honey
2 teaspoons ground ginger
1 tablespoon lemon juice
lemon rind cut in strips
toasted slivered almonds

Peel the pears, cut them in half lengthways and remove the core, or use whole, as desired. Place pears in a baking dish, cut side up. Cover with water, add sugar, cinnamon and cloves and poach until tender.

In a saucepan, mix together walnuts, dates, honey, ginger, lemon juice and rind. Add a little water and heat gently.

Serve pears with sauce, garnished with almonds.
Serves 4

ALMOND BANANA CREAM

2 bananas, peeled and sliced
2 teaspoons honey
½ cup ground almonds
6 strawberries

Wrap the banana slices in foil and freeze for 4 to 5 hours. Remove from the freezer and leave to stand for 5 minutes.

Put them in a blender with the honey, almonds and strawberries. Blend until they are pureed and serve immediately.
Serves 2

APPLE CRUMBLE

3 apples, peeled, cored and sliced
1 cup orange juice

Crumble
2 teaspoons butter
½ cup rolled oats
½ cup chopped almonds
2 teaspoons brown sugar
1 teaspoon ground cinnamon

Put the apples in a pan with the orange juice and cook over low heat for 15 minutes. Place into a cake tin or deep pie dish.

To make the crumble, melt the butter in a saucepan and add the oats, almonds, sugar and cinnamon.

Sprinkle the crumble on top of the stewed apples and bake at 180°C (350°F) for 20 minutes or until the topping is brown.
Serves 2

Fruit Brule

FRUIT BRULE

cups prepared fruit
cup cream
tablespoons brown sugar
¼ teaspoon cinnamon

Spun Toffee
½ cup sugar
water

Use any fruit in season for this dessert: grapes, peeled and seeded; cherries, seeded; apricots, quartered; strawberries, hulled; kiwi fruit, peeled and sliced.

Place the fruit into 4 individual ovenproof serving dishes and pour ¼ cup cream into each. Chill overnight.

Just before serving, sprinkle 1 tablespoon brown sugar and a little cinnamon over each and place under the griller until the sugar melts and browns. Garnish with spun toffee.

To make spun toffee, heat sugar in a saucepan. Brush edges with water using a pastry brush to dissolve crystals. Stir until sugar is dissolved. When toffee is boiling do not stir. Heat gently until a golden brown. It should be tacky when two spoons are touched together. Remove from the heat and spin toffee using spoons. Cut strands with scissors and arrange on top of fruit.
Serves 4

APRICOT AND NUT FLAN

Pastry
1 cup flour
2 tablespoons chopped almonds
2 tablespoons chopped walnuts
1 tablespoon sugar
40 g butter
1 egg
2 tablespoons lemon juice
iced water

Filling
425 g can apricot halves
2 tablespoons chopped dried apricots
4 tablespoons chopped almonds
1 egg yolk
2 egg whites
4 tablespoons sugar
extra apricot halves for decoration
(optional)

To make the pastry, place the flour, nuts and sugar in a bowl and rub in the butter with your fingertips. Mix together the egg and lemon juice and add to the flour mixture with enough iced water to form a firm dough. Wrap in plastic and chill for 20 minutes. Roll out the dough to fit an 18 cm flan tin. Chill while you prepare the filling.

Drain the apricots and puree them in a blender or strain through a sieve. Mix in the dried apricots, almonds and egg yolk. Beat the egg whites until stiff, add sugar and beat until it has dissolved. Fold into the apricot mixture and spoon into the pastry-lined flan tin. Bake at 180°C (350°F) for 1 hour. Decorate with extra apricot halves if desired.
Serves 6

RAINBOW RICE PUDDING

½ cup chopped pitted prunes
½ cup chopped dried apricots
½ cup chopped raisins
1 cup boiling water
juice ½ lemon
1 cup cooked brown rice
½ teaspoon nutmeg
½ teaspoon cinnamon
2 egg yolks
1 cup milk

Soak the fruit in the boiling water for 1 hour. Drain and add the lemon juice, mixing well. Mix the rice with the nutmeg, cinnamon, egg yolks and milk.

Starting and finishing with a rice layer, put alternate layers of fruit and rice in a well-greased souffle dish. Cover the dish and bake at 160°C (325°F) for 1 hour.

Remove from the oven and stand the dish in a pan of warm water for 10 minutes. Run a knife around the edge, and turn the pudding out onto a serving dish. Serve hot or cold.
Serves 4-6

TROPICAL SHERBET

1 cup fresh pineapple pieces
1 cup pawpaw or mango pieces
1 banana, chopped
½ cup orange juice
2 passionfruit
2 teaspoons honey

Place all the ingredients in a blender and blend until smooth. Pour it into an ice cream tray and freeze. Return the frozen mixture to the blender and blend again, just until it has a sorbet texture. If you blend for too long, it will become a liquid. Serve immediately, before it has time to thaw.
Serves 3

PEAR SHERBET

½ cup apple juice
2 pears, peeled and sliced
1 cup seedless grapes
1 cup peeled apple pieces
4 dates, stones removed
1 cup strawberries

Place all the ingredients in a blender and blend until smooth. Pour into an ice cream tray and freeze for 4 to 5 hours. Return the frozen fruit to the blender and blend again until it reaches the texture of sorbet. Serve immediately.
Serves 4

STEAMED APPLES IN FOIL

2 apples, cored and stuffed with dates or raisins
½ teaspoon honey or maple syrup

Cut out two 30 cm (12 inch) squares of foil and on each one arrange an apple with honey drizzled over. Wrap up well and steam in a steamer for 15 minutes. Serve hot.
Serves 2

MACERATED FRUITS

2 kg summer fruits, (pears, plums, strawberries, raspberries, cherries, apricots, bananas and peaches)
lemon juice
2 tablespoons honey
600 mL rose wine
yoghurt or cream, to serve

Prepare fruit and slice or halve according to size. Sprinkle lemon juice over any likely to brown (such as apples, pears or bananas). Layer fruit in large serving dish.

Stir honey into wine and pour over fruit. Leave overnight in refrigerator. Serve with yoghurt or cream.
Serves 6-8

PUMPKIN PIE

Pastry
1 cup self-raising flour
1 cup wholemeal flour
125 g butter
1 egg yolk
2 tablespoons lemon juice
iced water

Filling
350 g cooked pumpkin
1 tablespoon brown sugar
2 eggs, separated
4 tablespoons cream
¼ teaspoon nutmeg
¼ teaspoon ground ginger

To make the pastry, place the flours in a bowl and rub in the butter with your fingertips. Mix the egg yolk with the lemon juice, add to the flour mixture with enough iced water to make a smooth dough. Form into a ball, wrap in plastic and chill for 20 minutes. Roll out the dough, line a 20 cm pie dish and set aside in the refrigerator for 20 minutes.

Place the pumpkin in a blender or food processor with the sugar, egg yolks, cream, nutmeg and ginger. Blend to a puree. Beat the egg whites until stiff and fold into the pumpkin mixture. Pour into the pastry-lined pie dish and bake at 180°C (350°F) for 35 minutes or until the pastry is golden and the filling has set. Serve warm.
Serves 6

BAKED APPLE AND SAGO PUDDING

600 mL milk
¼ cup sago
3 eggs
2 tablespoons honey
⅛ teaspoon ground nutmeg
⅛ teaspoon ground cloves
2 apples peeled, cored and sliced
40 g butter

Bring milk and sago to boil and cook 8 minutes. Leave to cool. Beat in eggs, honey and spices. Gently cook apples in butter until soft. Arrange in souffle dish and fill dish with sago mixture. Place dish in baking tray half filled with hot water and bake at 180°C (350°F) for 45 minutes. Serve cold.
Serves 4

STRAWBERRY SORBET

1 punnet strawberries
1 cup water
¼ cup sugar
½ cup ice cream
2 tablespoons lemon juice
2 tablespoons Kirsch
2 egg whites
¼ cup caster sugar
extra whole strawberries, to garnish

Wash and hull the strawberries. Place them in a blender with the water, sugar, ice cream, lemon juice and Kirsch and puree. Pour the mixture into lamington tins and freeze.

Beat the egg whites until stiff, add the caster sugar and beat until dissolved. Remove the strawberry ice from the freezer and break up with a fork. Fold the egg whites into the strawberry mixture and spoon into individual serving bowls. Freeze, stirring every 10 minutes until the mixture is firm. When serving decorate with strawberries.
Serves 4

PEAR AND DATE CRUNCH

750 g pears, peeled and cored
250 g dates, halved and stoned
1 tablespoon raw sugar
½ teaspoon ground allspice
150 mL orange juice

Topping
125 g butter
1¼ cups wholemeal flour
¼ cup raw or brown sugar
½ cup rolled oats
½ teaspoon cinnamon

Cut pears into chunky pieces and place in ovenproof dish with dates, sugar, allspice and orange juice.

Rub butter into flour, stir in sugar oats and cinnamon. Sprinkle over fruit. Bake at 180°C (350°F) for 40 minutes until pears are soft and topping golden. Serve hot.
Serves 6

MENUS

LUNCH AND LIGHT MEALS

———

Potato Souffle
Mixed Salad
Fruit and Cheese

———

Cheesy Carrot Ring
Mixed Green Salad
Fruit

———

Chilled Pumpkin Soup
Farmhouse Salad

———

Eggplant and Walnut Puff
Green Salad

———

Vegetable Strudel
Mixed Green Salad

———

Spanakopita
Fresh Fruit

———

Vegetable Pate
Beef Cobbler
Green Salad

———

Vegetable Kebabs
Boiled Brown Rice
Chinese Pears

———

Potatoes Czarina
Green Salad
Fruit

———

Stuffed Artichokes
Apricot and Nut Flan

———

Seafood Pasta
Green Salad
Fruit

———

Iced Orange and Tomato Soup
Sesame Grilled Chicken
Mixed Salad

———

PARTY FOOD

———

Raw vegetables, cut into strips and
served with
Broad Bean Pate
Eggplant Puree
Prawn Pate

———

Hot Cheese Balls

———

Rice Croquettes with Tomato Sauce

———

Prawn Rascals

———

Potato Sticks

———

SLIMMING MENUS

———

Tomatoes Granita
Tofu Spinach Souffle
Fresh Fruit

———

Russian Red Cabbage Salad
Jewish Fish Balls

———

Iced Buttermilk Soup
Mixed Salad

———

Lemon Soup
Fresh Fruit

———

Fish Florentine
Fresh Fruit

———

Fish in Foil Packets
Mixed Salad
Fresh Fruit

———

RELAXED SUMMER DINNERS

———

Tomatoes Roquefort
Herbed Jellied Meat Loaf
Spicy Bean Sprouts

———

Iced Orange and Tomato Soup
Veal Parmigiana
Apricot Mousse

———

Cream of Choko Soup
Lamb and Nut Korma
Strawberry Sorbet

———

Iced Beetroot Soup
Broad Bean Casserole
Fruit Brule

———

Trout in Foil
Herbed Green Beans
Poached Peaches

———

Orange Chicken Parcels
Mixed Salad
Fruit Brule

———

Steamed Trout in Lime Butter
Green Salad
Fresh Fruit

———

Spicy Chicken Fillets
Brown Rice
Green Salad
Fresh Fruit

———

Grilled Marinated Fish
Tropical Sherbet

———

Vegetable Pate
Barramundi Kebabs

———

Fish Provencale
Steamed Apples in Foil

———

Chicken Hawaiian
Apricot Mousse

———

Clockwise from top: Fresh fruit and
cheese, Grilled Kingfish Cutlets, Green
Salad and Spanakopita

WINTER MENUS

Minestrone
Green Salad
Rainbow Rice Pudding

Stuffed Turnips
Apollo Steak
Glazed Brussels Sprouts
Ginger Souffle

Grilled Mushroom Caps
Eggplant Khoresh
Orange and Rhubarb Compote

Bean and Pea Soup
Green Salad
Pumpkin Pie

Cashew Nut Roast
Green Salad
Dried Fruit Crumble

Barley Vegetable Casserole
Green Salad

Fish Pie
Pear Sherbet

Baked Fish Casserole
Apple Crumble

Chicken Chasseur
Almond Banana Cream

LIGHT FAMILY MEALS

Fresh Tomato Soup
Zucchini and Cheese Salad
Fresh Fruit

Mughal Vegetables
Boiled Brown Rice
Pumpkin Pie

Curried Fish Risotto
Green Salad

Deep-fried Scallops and Prawns
Green Salad
Fresh Fruit

Soyaroni Cheese
Herbed Green Beans
Fresh Fruit

Spanish Omelette
Farmhouse Salad
Apricot Mousse

Baked Vegetable Ring with Tomato
Filling
Green Salad
Fresh Fruit

Watercress and Vermicelli Soup
Green Salad
Fruit and Cheese

Carrot and Orange Soup
Potato Souffle
Green Salad

Spanish-style Sardines
Vegetable Kebabs

Macaroni and Zucchini Salad
Spicy Peanut Roast Chicken

Chilled Green Pea Soup
Gemfish with Peanut Sauce

Spinach Tarts
Mixed Salad

Stir-fry Tofu
Mixed Salad
Fresh Fruit

Fish a la Grecque
Green Salad
Strawberry Sorbet

Curried Chicken
Brown Rice
Fresh Fruit

Baked Oriental Chicken
Orange and Rhubarb Compote

———

Chicken and Vegetable Stir-fry
Apple Crumble

———

Chicken Fillets with Tomato
Topping
Apricot Mousse

———

HIGH-FIBRE MENUS

Bean Salad
Fresh Fruit

———

Orange and Spinach Salad
Ribbon Bean Bake

———

Curried Brown Rice Salad
Provencale Chicken

———

Country Harvest Soup
Green Salad

Lentil Soup
Green Salad
Fresh Fruit

———

Braised Chinese Vegetables
Hungarian Bean and Vegetable
Loaf

———

MENUS FOR FITNESS

Fruit and Nut Salad
Pumpkin Pie

———

Tropical Rice Salad
Fresh Fruit

———

Lemon Soup
Zyldyk Casserole

———

Stir-fried Chicken
Mixed Salad

———

Cabbage Cake
Green Salad

———

Bean and Vegetable Tacos
Fruit

———

Minestrone
Green Salad

———

Chinese Green Soup
Poached Peaches

———

Crunchy Nut Terrine
Green Salad

———

Hot Rice Salad
Apricot and Nut Flan

———

QUICK MEALS

Instant Bean Medley
Green Salad

———

Melon Ambrosia

———

Gazpacho On Ice
Orange and Avocado Salad

———

Cold Yoghurt and Cucumber Soup
Grilled Kingfish Cutlets

———

Left to right: Watercress and Vermicelli
Soup, Sesame Grilled Chicken, Green
Salad and Poached Peaches

Glossary of Terms

AUSTRALIA	UK	USA
Equipment and terms		
aluminium foil	cooking foil	aluminium foil
can	tin	can
frying pan	frying pan	skillet
griller	grill	broiler
greaseproof paper	greaseproof paper	waxproof paper
lamington tin	ice-making tray	oven tray 1½" deep
paper towel	kitchen paper	white paper towel
patty tin	patty tin	muffin pan
plastic wrap	cling film	plastic wrap
punnet	punnet	basket for 250 g fruit
sandwich tin	sandwich tin	layer cake pan
seeded	stoned	pitted
Ingredients		
artichoke	globe artichoke	artichoke
bacon rasher	bacon rasher	bacon slice
beetroot	beetroot	beets
bicarbonate of soda	bicarbonate of soda	baking soda
black olive	black olive	ripe olive
Bok Choy	Pak Choi	Bok Choy
capsicum	pepper	sweet pepper
caster sugar	caster sugar	granulated table sugar
Chinese cabbage	Chinese leaves	Chinese cabbage
chuck steak	braising steak	chuck steak
converted rice	easy cook rice	converted rice
cornflour	cornflour	cornstarch
corn kernels	sweet corn	corn kernels
cream	single cream	light or coffee cream
desiccated coconut	desiccated coconut	shredded coconut
eggplant	aubergine	eggplant
plain flour	plain flour	all-purpose flour
gelatine	gelatine powder	gelatin
green cabbage	white or roundhead cabbage	cabbage
horseradish cream	horseradish sauce	horseradish
kidney beans	red kidney beans	kidney beans
light beer	lager	light beer
mutton	lamb	lamb
pawpaw	pawpaw	papaya or papaw
prawn	prawn or shrimp	shrimp
rockmelon	melon	cantaloupe
self-raising flour	self-raising flour	all-purpose flour with baking powder, 1 cup: 2 teaspoons
shallot	spring onion	scallion
snow pea	mangetout, sugar pea	snow pea
soybean	soyabean	soybean
stock cube	stock cube	bouillon
sugar pea or snap pea	snap beans	sugar pea or snap bean
sultanas	sultanas	seedless white or golden raisins
tasty cheese	mature Cheddar	Cheddar
thickened cream	double cream	heavy or whipping cream
tomato puree	tomato puree	tomato paste
tomato sauce	tomato sauce	tomato ketchup
veal scallops	veal escalops	veal
wholemeal flour	wholemeal flour	wholewheat flour
Worcestershire sauce	Worcester sauce	Worcestershire sauce
yeast extract (Vegemite)	Marmite	
yoghurt	natural yogurt	unflavoured yoghurt
zucchini	courgette	zucchini

Oven Temperatures

Celsius	Fahrenheit	
120	250	Very slow
140–150	275–300	Slow
160	325	Moderately slow
180	350	Moderate
190	375	Moderately hot
200	400	Hot
220	425	
230	450	
250–260	475–500	Very hot

Measurements

Standard Metric Measures

1 cup	=	250 ml
1 tablespoon	=	20 ml
1 teaspoon	=	5 ml

All spoon measurements are level

Cup Measures

1 × 250 mL cup =	Grams	Ounces
breadcrumbs, dry	125	4½
soft	60	2
butter	250	8¾
cheese, grated cheddar	125	4½
coconut, desiccated	95	3¼
flour, cornflour	130	4¾
plain or self-raising	125	4½
wholemeal	135	4¾
fruit, mixed dried	160	5¾
honey	360	12¾
sugar, caster	225	7¾
crystalline	250	8¾
icing	175	6¾
moist brown	170	6
nuts	125	4

If you need to substitute

Fresh fruit: replace with canned or tinned fruit.
Fresh herbs: replace with a quarter of the recommended quantity of dried herbs.
Fresh dill: replace with fresh parsley.
Snake beans: replace with fresh haricot or French beans.
Soybeans: replace with haricot or borlotti beans.
Ginger root: replace with preserved ginger.

Almond meal: replace with ground almonds.
Smoked fish: replace with fish such as smoked haddock.
Snapper or bream: replace with sea bream, bass or any firm white flesh fish including cod, whiting or haddock.
Barramundi or gemfish: replace with monkfish or whiting.
1 bunch spinach — stalk and leaves: weighs approx. 1.2 kg.
1 bunch of rhubarb — stalk and leaves: weighs approx. 1 kg.

INDEX